JOHN PETER ZENGER
AND THE
FUNDAMENTAL FREEDOM

William Lowell Putnam

with a foreword by
Paul Sweitzer

D1246692

McFarland & Company, Inc., Publishers
Jefferson, North Carolina, and London

British Library Cataloguing-in-Publication data are available

Library of Congress Cataloguing-in-Publication Data

Putnam, William Lowell.
    John Peter Zenger and the fundamental freedom / William Lowell
Putnam ; with a foreword by Paul Sweitzer.
       p.   cm.
    Includes bibliographical references and index.
    ISBN 0-7864-0370-5 (library binding : 50# alkaline paper) ∞
    1. Zenger, John Peter, 1697–1746 — Trials, litigation, etc.
2. Trials (Seditious libel) — New York (State) — New York.   3. Freedom
of the press — United States — History.   4. Publishers and publishing —
New York (State) — Biography.   5. Newspaper publishing — New York
(State) — History.   I. Title.
KF223.Z4P87   1997
342.73'0853 — dc21   97-14213
                                                      CIP

*No part of this book, specifically including the table of contents and index,
may be reproduced or transmitted in any form or by any means, electronic
or mechanical, including photocopying or recording, or by any information
storage and retrieval system, without permission in writing from the
publisher.*

Manufactured in the United States of America

*McFarland & Company, Inc., Publishers
  Box 611, Jefferson, North Carolina 28640*

John Peter Zenger
and the Fundamental Freedom

for Richard Conrad Garvey,
my competitor, my inspiration
and my friend

Table of Contents

List of Illustrations

All illustrations are from the collection of the New-York Historical Society and are reproduced here by their kind permission.

Acknowledgments

This effort to place the trial and vindication of John Peter Zenger in a perspective useful to the citizenry more than 250 years later has been aided by a number of good people. Among them are Andrew John Kauffman, with whom I have shared a close friendship for more than half a century; Richard Garvey, a monumental journalistic archive in his own right; Paul Peter Nicolai, who gave me the initial legal references; Wayman Lee, who steered me around the law library of the city of Springfield; and Joseph Pessolano, who also held my hand during an earlier moment of crisis. Credit belongs in addition with the scholarly and gracious printers at Old Sturbridge Village, Carl Austin and William Contino; to my younger and classically inclined brother, Michael, for his helpful translations; to Charles A. Carroll for some interesting tidbits; and to various polite people at several facilities, the extensive law library of Western New England College, the public library of Springfield, the Robert Frost Library of Amherst College and the library of the University of Massachusetts.

Especial thanks are due to Paul Sweitzer, another walking journalistic archive, whose diaskeuastical review sharpened my focus in critical areas and whose foreword adds distinction to this endeavor, and to my erudite granddaughter, Eleanor, who sacrificed much of a cherished vacation to improving my syntax and grammar. Much essential help has also been graciously given by the New York Historical Society through Debra Randorf.

The courage of Peter Zenger is in the nature of journalistic folklore in the United States; the story of his imprisonment, trial and vindication was widely reported at the time and his own subsequent account has been republished in dozens of American newspapers, and even in Europe. In the years that have followed, many scholars have commented on various aspects of the case from which the recitation of sources herein is culled. However, an exhaustive list of peripheral material can be found in the 1963 volume entitled *A Brief Narrative of the Case and Trial of John Peter Zenger* by James Alexander, edited by Stanley Nider Katz and published by Harvard University Press. While I strongly disagree with Katz's position that Zenger was merely a pawn at the time — and a rather irrelevant one in history, at that — his research was thorough. As a sometime practicing journalist who has been threatened with jail for not revealing sources, I have a great regard for Zenger's courage in serving his time rather than tattling on his sources, who were the real targets of Governor Cosby's attention. This is a fundamental point that Katz overlooks. Rather than reprint Katz's scholarly notations, they are hereby duly referenced and the serious student should seek out the volume. Many issues of Zenger's newspaper are to be found in the archives of the New York Public Library and the New York Historical Society, as are copies of some of the colonial correspondence that bears on his trial and on the events which led up to it. Most of the commentary on Zenger's trial has tended to concentrate on the lead-in and the trial, its social and legal implications at the time, not on its fundamental and far-reaching nature as a landmark in the total quest for individual liberties. John Peter Zenger may well have been an "indifferent printer," by any definition of the word, but he was a journalist's journalist of the finest order — he could have walked out of jail any time, if he had only been willing to identify his sources.

Therefore, it is not out of place to express thanks, for their setting of the stage for America's unique *First Amendment,* to the organizers of history's first recorded work stoppage on Rome's Aventine Hill; to the unknown draftsmen (for I am guessing that they were all of the male gender) who framed the *Magna Carta*; to their descendants more than a dozen generations later who framed the English *Bill of Rights*; to the great British stimulators of thought, Addison, Steele, Locke, Trenchard and Gordon; to Thomas Jefferson, the slaveowner who drew up mankind's most passionate exposition of the right to freedom; and to Abbé Sieyès, who drafted the *Declaration of the Rights of Man and of the Citizen.* They all created legal landmarks in the quest for freedom of expression as the most fundamental of human rights, but it remained for Dr. Ralph D. Abernathy to formulate the latest interpretation of those rights in the name of his collaborator, Dr. Martin Luther King, Jr., and they both deserve everyone's thanks as well.

Foreword
The First Stone in the Bulwark
by Paul Sweitzer

For the almost four decades that I took paychecks in journalism, I rarely thought about the freedom I enjoyed. Like most of my brethren, I accepted that freedom and protested only when I thought it threatened. The First Amendment to the U.S. Constitution has stood for two centuries. It is one of the most remarkable statements of intent in human history, guaranteeing the unconditional right to freedom of thought and expression.

Recently I talked with a British friend who reminded me, bluntly, "Here in the States, people just don't understand that the press in England is *not* free!" He is right. There are many regulations, written and unwritten, governing the conduct of writers in virtually every other country of the world. Of course, there are ideas, precedents, regulations and even laws aimed at such governance in this country, too, but never in a blunt, overt way.

Here, you can publish anything you want about anyone you want. There is the accepted precaution that what you publish should be the truth — or at least be what you honestly perceive to be truth. Television magazine shows and grocery store tabloids pretty much conclusively prove that in application this precaution is mostly theoretical. American journalism, from the first, has been guided by this axiom: "If you can get someone to say it, publish it. If not, say it yourself, label it 'opinion' or 'analysis,' and *then* publish it."

What is the source of such freedom?

In this book, William Lowell Putnam recalls the often-forgotten story of an otherwise obscure printer and publisher who was willing to fight for the freedom of expression and who paid a price that his successors might be free.

1

From 1734 to 1735, John Peter Zenger spent nine months in jail in colonial New York because he dared print things in his *New York Weekly Journal* that defied and displeased the colony's royal governor. Zenger's case was not all that unusual. In Boston, in the 1690s, Benjamin Harris, publisher of this nation's first newspaper, *Publick Occurrences Both Forreign and Domestick*, was arrested by royal authorities, and his newspaper was shut down after only one issue.

Zenger and his supporters fought back. Eventually, a jury ruled it was Zenger's right to expose the activities of the governor and his cronies; thus was established a great precedent for American freedom of expression. The ruling won by Zenger's attorney was the first major victory in America in an on-going, never-ending fight for this freedom, which has carried out, at continual cost, by some of history's most famous figures.

Socrates paid with his life for freedom of expression in 399 B.C. The rulers of Athens condemned the rugged, old teacher to death by hemlock because he expressed ideas not up to the standard of "uncritical patriotism" established for Athenians by their leaders. Of course, those leaders did not have the courage to charge Socrates with that. He was condemned for "corrupting the youth" and "impiety." Individuals and groups in this country still use those reasons to try to proscribe music, books, plays, motion pictures and even journalism.

In 1633, the Italian mathematician Galileo was sentenced to life imprisonment because he espoused ideas opposing those of the Roman church, arguing that Earth is not a fixed body at the center of the universe. The sentence was commuted to house arrest in his own villa, but Galileo's writings and teachings were proscribed for the rest of his life.

The Nazis' treatment of such revered figures as Thomas Mann and Franz Werfel during the 1930s and the Soviet Union's treatment of poet and novelist Boris Pasternak during the 1950s are more recent examples of such stifling of the freedom of expression.

Such attempts continue, even in this country, where the First Amendment is an absolute guarantee of such freedom. Every day some journalist or critic, somewhere, is taken to task by some elected official, bureaucrat, government entity or interest group because that person has dared to publish something the offended party disliked. Criminal charges are not filed in such cases, but great pressures, of many other kinds, are regularly brought to bear.

John Peter Zenger did his job, and the government tried to stop him. It would have been easy for him to have backed down, but he and his supporters did not choose that route. It is a fascinating story. Putnam brings it alive again after more than two centuries, telling much of it in Zenger's own words. The author describes a time in America when learning a trade or profession was not a matter of a few years of school followed by a glibly served "internship." Such preparation in colonial times was a matter of as many as ten years of virtual slavery in the form of indentured apprenticeship. If the apprentice survived, he was ready for the world. Zenger did so and became a respected figure in his community and, almost unwittingly, a hero. Perhaps the rigors of apprenticeship helped build a character that allowed him to achieve a place in history.

Without Zenger, without his trial, the people and the legislatures of the original states might not have been so insistent that the Founding Fathers add to their original work a provision that forever guaranteed the freedoms the royal governors had tried so hard to curtail: "Congress shall make no law respecting an establishment of religion or prohibiting the free exercise thereof; or abridging the freedom of speech or of the press; or the right of the people peaceably to assemble and to petition the government for a redress of grievances."

That's our First Amendment — all forty-four words of it. Its noble intentions have been vigorously battered, even abused by some, for many years. But it stands, history's greatest bulwark against tyranny. John Peter Zenger laid a great foundation stone in that bulwark.

Recite that amendment aloud. Think, then, about what you have said. It has a grand ring and is worth thinking about and defending every day of your life.

Paul Sweitzer, a reportorial jack-of-all-trades on the staff of the Arizona Daily Sun, *the community newspaper of Flagstaff, Arizona, for 36 years, is a freelance writer and community activist in Flagstaff.*

Preface

John Peter WHO?

Why should an English-speaking nation owe its greatest debt to a German-born "indifferent printer" whose main claim to fame is the amount of trouble he got into?

By way of answer to this question, near the start of his eventful life in service to the United States of America, Gouverneur Morris wrote, "The trial of Zenger in 1735 was the germ of American freedom, the morning star of that liberty which subsequently revolutionized America."

We should first note that the adjective "indifferent" must be understood in the context of an earlier era. Words change in their meanings, as any lexicographer will attest; in the original edition of Noah Webster's opus *A Compendious Dictionary of the English Language* (1806), one finds the word defined primarily as "unconcerned, regardless, impartial, equal" — a far cry from today's primary usage as "mediocre, passable, apathetic."

The United States Constitution went into effect on 3 March 1789, completely replacing the eight-year-old Articles of Confederation, whose clause requiring unanimity before any action could be taken had severely hampered any effective group action. The Confederation's other flaws, while democratically induced and thus presumably meritorious, had done almost as much to hinder the success of the War for Independence as had the British. Approval of the new Federal arrangement had passed in the requisite nine of the original states the previous 21 June, when New Hampshire gave its assent. Delaware, the most vulnerable of the confederated states, had been the first to accept and ratify the new constitution on 7 December 1787, less than three months after its approval by the Congress. In 1787 and 1788 other states followed in order: Pennsylvania (where the framers had met) on 12 December,

New Jersey on 18 December, Georgia on 2 January, Connecticut on 9 January, Massachusetts (by a slim margin) on 28 April and South Carolina on 21 June. After New Hampshire's critical approval, Virginia came along on 26 June, New York a month later, North Carolina on 21 November and finally Rhode Island (which had sent no delegate to the framing convention) on 10 January 1791. By this time, Vermont had settled its border dispute with New York and already been admitted as the fourteenth state.

However, in several cases the ratifying state conventions had done so only after their representatives to the Congress had been instructed to give prompt attention to a series of amendments — to be known collectively almost immediately as the American Bill of Rights. Those initial and mostly personal rights have often been cited, often been litigated, sometimes been ignored and frequently abused. But collectively they remain the cornerstone of American ideals respecting individual human rights, and they glow as a beacon of hope that continues to draw thousands of freedom lovers every year to the land of individual opportunity engendered by their guarantees.

The people of America are no different from others in other corners of the globe and in other periods of history. They are born just as short-sighted, ambitious and self-centered as the ancestors and cousins they left behind. In addition, many of the more immediate forebears of modern Americans have sinned grievously against the original tenants of this "land of liberty," given scant welcome to quite a few of those who have flocked to America's banner of freedom and in many cases inflicted incalculable and long-lasting injury on the very land of the republic. Total fairness, however, has never been a characteristic of any political system, no matter how much people have tried to achieve it.

But, for all of America's well-cited shortcomings, its political pioneers built well and, perhaps inadvertently, not only provided for the perpetuation of their ideals, but for their proliferation as well. They based their own freedom and that of their successors on a small but far-reaching number of personal guarantees — starting with the right to complain: to think, speak and write one's piece without fear of losing life or liberty. No other nation in the world or throughout human history has made that concept a fundamental and absolute part of its political and social system. America's First Amendment is unique.

It was a belief in the freedom to publish his views of truth that enabled Samuel Adams to inspire his fellow citizens against the tyranny of taxation without representation. It was a belief in the freedom to speak his views of truth that enabled Patrick Henry to utter his stirring cry to action in defense of liberty. It was a belief in the freedom to vent an honestly held opinion that gave Thomas Jefferson the courage to address His Britannic Majesty in the deathless — even if slightly inaccurate — prose of our Declaration of Independence.

American freedom to speak and to publish the truth first became a reality in 1735. In that year Scottish-born Andrew Hamilton successfully reached into the depths of the common law to convince a jury of his peers that his client, John Peter Zenger, the German-born, thirty-eight-year-old publisher of the *New York Weekly Journal*, should bear no guilt and pay no penalty for having written and published factually — if unwelcomely — about the actions and associates of William Cosby, His Majesty George II's governor of New York.

After 1790, American freedoms became legendary around the world. They brought men and women of intellectual ferment to this land above all others, and with those individuals came amazing economic progress. They have also allowed the world's fullest expression of human faiths, hopes and follies. And the foremost of those freedoms has always assured the full light of scrutiny — welcome or not — on the acts of our government. It all began on that day when Peter Zenger walked from jail, free to resume his public exposure of what officialdom viewed as distasteful.

This book is not a eulogy of an "indifferent printer," nor does it purport to be the complete story of a displaced German, immigrant to the province of New York. It is an attempt to set forth, in relatively concise form, his actions and tribulations in the context of the evolution of free speech and other precious human liberties.

Americans, in our land of plenty and freedom of expression, tend to take many things for granted. But, conscious of our freedom or not, we are unanimously able to articulate our criticisms, caring little that they always be accurate, tasteful or timely. That freedom to criticize, indeed, is what has given us our plenty, for we do not have to accept without complaint the wisdom of any entrenched bureaucrat. In addition, the openness and robust divergence among American news media gives all views an opportunity to be heard — even the wrong and mean-spirited. It is that freedom which makes all the difference.

Most citizens of the United States do not realize how unique we are among nations of the world. Though our news media are often accused of holding common biases, we take for granted that there is competition among them and that they are free to disseminate whatever their proprietors or employees may think worthwhile. And this has been increasingly true in recent years as the electronic media have become ever more deregulated. But, what is also true is that this condition of unhampered communication does not pertain quite so strongly elsewhere. In Western Europe, to a large extent, such freedom does exist; but as one gets farther away from the centers of traditional political freedom this condition becomes less true and the news media tend to become more and more "official"—meaning by this, "government controlled."

To some peoples, this condition of "ignorance" has been acceptable—even normal—for they have never existed under any other effective form of information delivery. Perhaps, more than any other factor, the *Voice of America* began to change that global complacency by consistently attempting to deliver to all peoples, in all languages, a consistent and alternative source of news and information to what was officially sanctioned by other countries' rulers.

During the waning years of the Soviet Union, this writer had his eyes opened to the complacency with which many people elsewhere in the world could accept censorship of news and the consequent stifling of expression. After Mikhail Gorbachev had begun to allow diverse voices to appear in that nation, among the better educated Soviet citizens there began an increasing freedom of dialogue with visiting foreigners. During my first visit to the international high-angle climbing competitions in the Crimea, I was shunned as a representative of American imperialism — treated politely because of my interest in what had heretofore been an exclusively Russian sport, but very definitely not welcomed into anyone's inner thoughts. Three years later, during my second such visit, I was amazed at the freedom with which all my hosts were now complaining about the sad state of the Soviet system and economy.

These were typical comments: "There is nothing worth buying in the stores"; "I have to wait seven years to buy a new car, and then it's junk"; "Will you sell me your climbing rope? We can't get anything like that here"; "This country is awful; and Gorbachev is responsible." And so it went, often in lurid and personal detail. This was a far different condition from my earlier visit, during which I heard no adverse comment about anything, even though all the facts were just as obvious to the intelligent observer.

In trying to match the new-found effusiveness of my hosts, I remonstrated, telling these now freely griping friends that they did not realize how great a step their country had taken towards the economic plenty that they were searching for. "Don't gripe about Gorbachev,"

I pleaded; "he has given you the most useful gift of all. Now you can complain openly. It may take a few years [perhaps I should have said 'decades'], but everything else you want will come along in due course."

I

Young Peter

Zenger's Background and Environment

Although there had been some tentative steps towards a better defined concept of individual human liberties over the previous centuries, particularly in England, it is in the eighteenth century that this narrative more properly starts — in the then "petty princeling" state of Germany called the Upper Palatinate (*Ober Pfalz* in German). This area, a part of modern Bavaria largely north of the Danube, derived its name, as well as the general term for its residents, from the name of its rulers who were titled "Count Palatine" by virtue of their hereditary and independent status within the Holy Roman Empire.[1]

Central Germany had been the principal battleground of the Thirty Years War (1618–48) and following that, of the War of the Spanish Succession (which did not get finally settled until 1713). Compounding the ravages inflicted as a condition of central Germany's war-zone status, the 1648 Treaty of Westphalia — which both settled a lot of things and left a lot pending — had included the restatement of a unique clause that specified the future existence locally of three, and only three, religions: Catholic, Lutheran and Calvinist.[2] While this clause might have indicated a degree of religious toleration, that condition was diminished substantially by a further clause specifying that the religion practiced by each independent ruler would also be that of his subjects.[3] Since 1685, the ruler of the Palatinates had been a Catholic, John William, Duke of Neuburgh, one of the nine electors of the Holy Roman Emperor. Many of his subjects, however, were of a different persuasion concerning the better route to eternal salvation.

The harsh winter of 1708–1709 brought many Europeans to think of more earthly concerns. All Europe was caught in the clutches of fearsome and unprecedented cold — the most difficult stretch of an era known to later historians as "the Little Ice Age" (caused by the lengthy period of low sunspot activity later identified as "the Maunder Minimum"). After October, it was said that firewood could not be burned in the open air, that wine and other spirits froze, that human spittle hit the ground frozen, that birds on the wing fell dead from the sky. The Rhône River was frozen over, and heavily laden carts could be hauled along the shore ice of the North Sea. Small wonder there were refugees — displaced persons fleeing a war zone, a ruler intolerant of their consciences and a climate that killed.

By the springtime of 1709, the refugees were embarking for the more tolerant — to Protestants anyway — climate of England. They brought with them a taste for beer, a foreign tongue and little else. Consequently, like all other refugees before and since, they received an uncertain welcome, living in "tent cities" on the outskirts of society. Queen Anne, a practical ruler but compassionate at heart, tried to move them on to places where they could earn their way and lead their lives, but with minimal disruption to her realm. Having lived through the shifting persecutions of her era, this last Stuart did see some merit in assisting persecuted humans to exit from areas of intolerance to regions where they might more readily be free to think and worship as they pleased. Thus, some of the refugee Palatines were settled in Ireland, where unfortunately their un–Roman religion made them suspect — compelling this group, after two unhappy generations, to migrate again, this time to upper Canada. Most of the displaced Palatines, however, were sent directly on a transatlantic voyage, to the now totally British colonies of New York,[4] New Jersey and Pennsylvania.[5]

They were counted and analyzed by a number of observers. According to Daniel Defoe's arithmetic in his 1709 *Brief History of the Poor Palatine Refugees Lately Arrived in England*, the first group, which arrived in England between 1 May and 18 July 1709, totalled some 6,500 persons: 1,278 men having families, 1,234 wives, 89 widows, 384 unmarried men, 106 unmarried women, 379 boys above age fourteen, 374 girls above age fourteen, 1,367 boys under age fourteen and 1,309 girls under age fourteen. Defoe further grouped these into thirty-two different occupations: 1,083 husbandmen and vinedressers, 4 herdsmen, 10 schoolmasters, 13 wheelwrights, 46 smiths, 66 weavers, 90 carpenters, 32 bakers, 48 masons and so on, even down to 2 carvers, 1 cook and 1 student.

The name "Zenger" might appear to derive from Zinger the Middle High German nickname for a lively person. As such its family seat would be in the Bernese Oberland, centered around Meiringen.[6] But that is a genealogical red herring: various extant Palatinate records indicate a different geographical origin and a different patronymic derivation.

The most pertinent such record reveals that the third refugee ship arriving in London from Rotterdam in the summer of 1709 carried Nicolaes Zingeler (aged forty) with his wife, Johanna, and four children. At year's end, the London records of "Red House" show the residency of Nicholas Eberhard Zenger and family. Then began the crowded, two-month-long, unsanitary and tragedy-ridden voyage across the ocean. In New York, on Governor Robert Hunter's list of 30 June 1710, one can find only Johanna Zangerin with two dependents over age ten and three under that age.[7] Nicholas had died on the ocean voyage. By year's end, Johanna Zenger is listed as a widow (aged thirty-three) with sons, Peter (aged thirteen) and Johannes (aged seven), and a daughter, Anna Catherina (aged ten).

Quite a few of the Palatine immigrants were unhappy with their enforced surroundings, first on Governor's Island and then in various degrees of servitude to earlier settlers. Among their complaints were that they were denied sufficient beer and that parents were being separated from their families. As a result many Palatines worked their way northward to unsettled lands in present-day Dutchess County and established communities with names that reminded them of their homeland — New Paltz and Newburgh. Johanna Zenger, however, stuck it out in New York, and her older son became one of the seventy-four immigrant children indentured or apprenticed by Governor Robert Hunter to a variety of New York City businessmen. On 26 October 1710, she signed the articles of indenture for her eldest son as an apprentice for the next eight years to William Bradford (1663–1752), soon to become the official printer for the Province of New York.[8]

Indentured servitude as a way of survival was a time-honored practice in the American colonies. A deal was struck whereby the master — be he a craftsman with a trade or a farmer with land — undertook to teach the indentured servant the trade, provide him or her (generally "him") with room, board and clothing, and perhaps pay for his voyage across the ocean and other expenses. The time period of this servitude varied with each case, but generally ranged from five to ten years. By this system, parents could relieve themselves of responsibility for children they simply could not otherwise support, and the master could get a reliable source of cheap labor for awhile. These arrangements worked out fairly well for the most part — though some indentured servants were treated little better than slaves, others grew up to marry the boss's daughter, as had Bradford. Writing a few years later, Dirch Ten Broeck told of studying the law under the tutelage of Alexander Hamilton with "unremitting application," but also complained that his apprenticeship

Robert Hunter, captain general and governor-in-chief of the province of New York

had required "the sacrifice of every pleasure." Young Peter seems to have learned the printing trade effectively enough, and he remained on sufficiently good terms with Bradford to return, albeit only for two years, as his partner. Printing, in the days before the invention of mechanical and electronic typesetting devices, was a highly skilled trade, requiring great attention to detail and considerable training.

Bradford, the progenitor of a long and distinguished line of American printers, was a man of many accomplishments. A Quaker immigrant from Barnwell in Leicestershire, he had learned his trade in England as an apprentice under the tutelage of Andrew Sowles, a Quaker who had been shunned in some circles because of his faith. Bradford had made an initial journey "to the colonies" in 1682 and, in 1685, settled permanently in Philadelphia, where he established that city's first printing press. Five years later, mostly with the help of the German-born Mennonite preacher William Rittenhouse (1644–1708), he built — on the banks of Paper Mill Run in Roxborough Township — the first paper mill in the colonies. After a decade of operation, during which Bradford transferred his interest to the Rittenhouse family, the mill was washed out by a flood; it was rebuilt in 1702, relocated slightly downstream to safer terrain and, after 1708, run by Klass Rittenhouse, son of the founder. Bradford, though removed from Pennsylvania, was for many subsequent years, the largest (and sometimes the only) purchaser of the mill's output.

Bradford's press was the third — and most controversial of the three — to be established in the North American colonies. The first was in Cambridge, Massachusetts, in 1638, and was operated somewhat as an adjunct to Harvard College.[9] Since, in those days, the college was generally regarded as a creature of the commonwealth — or of its religious establishment — this press was considered "safe" from a political point of view. The second North American printing establishment was set up in 1674 in Boston, just across the river from the first. It, too, was in safe hands, since it was largely under the control of the crown's minion, the colonial postmaster.

Bradford had lost favor with various Pennsylvania authorities in 1692 for printing the works of George Keith, who had charged that the Quaker colony's officials were not being consistent with Friends' principles when they outfitted and *armed* several vessels in an effort to suppress piracy.[10] Bradford, though merely the printer of Keith's polemics, was condemned locally under the catchall offense of seditious libel. In his defense Bradford had argued, unsuccessfully, that truth freed him from the charge of libel. Unfortunately, in matters of religion, truth has always been a matter of controversy or controversy's early casualty, creating countless martyrs and causing innumerable wars. Bradford's defense was a good try, but clearly somewhat ahead of the times. Bradford was not imprisoned, but his press and inventory were confiscated — a severe financial blow. Understandably, he thought his prospects might be better elsewhere and, upon the invitation of Governor Benjamin

Fletcher,[11] moved to New York the following year. There he set up shop, the only printer in town at that time. Fletcher, who had wished to have his own record regarding Indian affairs made more public, was quick to appoint Bradford the official printer for the province and saw to it that his press and fonts were returned to him.

In the same year, 1718, that Zenger completed his indenture, his master's younger son, Andrew Sowles Bradford (1686–1742), named for his maternal grandfather, returned to Philadelphia to become postmaster and to produce the first Pennsylvania newspaper, the *American Weekly Mercury*. Only coincidentally, this publication was to have a peripheral relationship to the outcome of Zenger's trial in 1735. It must have been a good business, for Andrew's nephew, another William Bradford (1722–1791), established a competing entity in 1742, the *Weekly Advertiser, or Pennsylvania Journal,* which played a vigorous antiestablishment role in opposing the Stamp Act. William earned the gratitude of the Continental Congress for his editorial courage and became its official printer, while his son, yet another William, became Attorney General of the fledgling United States of America. Andrew Bradford as well earned a small niche in history, when he gave shelter (but not employment) to America's most famous printer when the seventeen-year-old and penniless Benjamin Franklin arrived in Philadelphia in 1723.[12]

Eighteenth-century print shops were a lot different from those of modern times, where one delivers a floppy disc and in ten minutes can take away a bundle of finished brochures. In those first print shops, overhead were racks to hold the newly printed sheets and the ever-present peel, with which the printer carefully lifted each page to rest overnight while the costly pine rosin, linseed oil and carbon-black ink took its own sweet time to dry (generally up to eighteen hours). Along one wall were shelves to hold the printer's "wood furniture," quoins, chases, composing sticks and mallets — the tools with which type was set into its desired galley form. In numerous shallow bins and drawers, all placed for ease of access, were found the assorted varieties of type, ornate bordering dies and blank slugs that constituted the printer's major capital investment necessary to produce the varied styles sought by his customers. High-speed operation, in those days of hand-driven machinery, meant a maximum of 250 impressions per hour (on one side of the sheet only). Over all this presided the master printer, invariably dressed in his wide-skirted and often ink-stained smock. His press stood in one corner, its movable bed containing the composition in process, while close by was the inking stand and deerskin-sheathed roller bully with which the assembled form was periodically refreshed. While the master printer may well have gone home (generally upstairs over the shop) with his hands covered in ink and his smock stained, his apprentice or assistant was soon given the name of "devil" because he was so often completely covered with black. The apprentice not only ran errands and delivered the finished products, but he also mixed the ink from the jars of raw material kept in a handy closet.

Having served out his indenture by 1719, Zenger migrated southward, and in that year, on 28 July, he married Mary White of Philadelphia. Settling in Kent County on Maryland's eastern shore, he set out to achieve recognition and was awarded the privilege of printing the acts of the assembly sessions, for which he was paid five hundred pounds of tobacco. However, Mary's early death left him with an infant son and a number of unhappy memories. Zenger thereupon returned to the greater economic opportunities of New York, where, on 11 September 1722, he married Anna Catherina Maulin (1704–1751), who turned out to be a lady of considerable courage and loyalty and by whom he later had an additional five children. In 1723, Zenger had accumulated sufficient real property to become a "freeman" of the city, thus joining the voters for provincial elections and enjoying full citizenship privileges.

In 1725, William Bradford accepted his former apprentice as a partner. However, the partnership soon dissolved when Zenger opened his own printing establishment on Smith (now William) Street in 1726. From that location and from a subsequent shop on Broad Street, for the next several years he printed various tracts — what would later have been called "position papers" — and miscellaneous theological works. But in 1730, Zenger printed America's first textbook on arithmetic, an English-language version of the Dutch scholar Peter Venema's *Arithmetica*. In 1733 Zenger began publishing his *New York Weekly Journal*.

Zenger had established his own print shop while Bradford was investing in a paper mill at Elizabethtown, New Jersey, to help supply his newly established *New York Gazette*. The *Gazette* was the first weekly newspaper in that colony and the fifth such publication in North America, the first having been the *Publick Occurrences, Both Forreign and Domestick*, published in Boston in 1690 by Benjamin Harris.[13] Harris, however, was sufficiently ahead of his time in disseminating his version of important events that his journal was suppressed, and he was imprisoned after its very first issue. Governor Simon Bradstreet, in ordering this unlicensed paper out of business, had noted that it contained "reflections of a very high nature" as well as "sundry doubtful and uncertain reports."[14] In the printed announcement of the suppression, the governor and his council proclaimed their "high Resentment and Disallowance" and forbade anyone else to set anything into print without prior consent. This process of control was lawful in the colonies until 1730, even though such laws were no longer in effect in England after the Glorious Revolution.[15]

Bradford, remembering his own earlier difficulties with official intolerance and obviously wanting little of that in the future, established his weekly newspaper as the official organ of the colonial government. As printer to the royal appointees, at an annual salary of £50 plus the title of "King's Printer to the Province of New York," Bradford and his *Gazette* were thoroughly "safe." In fact, when the political firestorm struck a few years later, Bradford avoided any editorial role, remaining merely the printer — as did Zenger. Both of them, however, in their capacities as publishers, were strongly supplemented by writers and editors supplied by their respective backers. The *Gazette*'s editor was Francis Harison, clerk of the province and a toady for the royal governor; Harison was as personally avaricious as his master, but more on the scale of a petty larcenist. [16] Because of his other questionable activities, he turned out to be as much of a liability as an asset. Furthermore, as the record clearly shows, at the moment it counted, Zenger's *Journal* had by far the better editorial staff.

Bradford was having other troubles, too; though he had trained many of the subsequently independent printers of the middle colonies, not all his apprentices were as loyal and honorable as Zenger had been. One of them, who later became a printer of some consequence (see Chapter XII), had compelled Bradford to run the following notice in the *Gazette* on 23 May 1733:

> Ran away on the 17th of this Instant *May*, from the Printer hereof, an Apprentice Lad, named James Parker, by Trade a Printer, aged about 19 years; he is of fresh complection, with short yellowish hair, having on a yellowish Bengall Coat, Jacket and Breeches, lined with the same, and has taken with him a brown colour'd coarse Coat, with flat Metal Buttons, Two Frocks, Two Shirts, One Pair of strip'd Ticken Jacket and Breeches. Whoever takes up and secures the said Apprentice, so that his said Master may have him again, shall have *Twenty Shillings* as a Reward, and all reasonable Charges Paid by
> WILLIAM BRADFORD

Since the members of the Governor's Council were to figure prominently in the later life and principal fame of Zenger, it is important to understand their relationship to the governor and the people. A concise analysis of this body was offered by Edgar Werner in 1888[17]:

> The Council of the Governor of the Colony of New York does not
> seem to have been, at first, limited to any determinate number....
> [I]n 1691, the number was increased to twelve, and so remained
> fixed whilst the English possessed the country, though by death and
> other casualties it sometimes fell short of that number. All the members
> rarely attended the sittings of the Council, many residing at a
> distance. They were named in the Governor's instructions, but
> vacancies were filled, from time to time, either by the Governor, or
> by royal mandamus....[18]
> Their functions were threefold: 1. In an Executive capacity, they
> acted as a Privy Council to the head of Government in civil matters,
> who was generally present when the Executive Council was in
> session. They were consulted in the grant of all [land] patents, which
> could not pass the seal without their advice; they also had a voice
> in the appointment to most of the civil offices in the colony. 2. They
> constituted the second branch of the Legislature, co-ordinate with
> the Senate of the present day.... At first the Chief Justice presided,
> but his duties at the Supreme Court requiring his attendance, it
> was resolved that the senior councillor present should be President....
> When acting as Legislative Councillors, their proceedings
> were very formal, and in many respects they imitated the House of
> Lords. Each member had the privilege of entering his dissent, and
> the reason at large on the minutes, but could not vote by proxy....
> A Councillor's title was "The Honorable." ... He held his office
> during pleasure and served without salary. His position, nevertheless,
> was such, that he was enabled to secure for himself, his family
> and friends, large grants of land, which indemnified him for whatever
> time and labor he otherwise lost.

It can therefore be appreciated that the average resident of the
colony hardly felt the members of this body to be reliably defending
their interests. One can assume that, given a chance, the members of
the public groused about the privileged upper class and would welcome
a chance to take them down a peg. Though not as virulent as in other
colonies, the state of public opinion in New York was such that whoever
might cause embarrassment to this group, or its leader, would be
something of a popular hero.

And so it was that in 1733, backed by a number of influential local
businessmen, each with his own reasons for wishing to influence pub-

lic opinion, Zenger brought out his "seditious" newspaper, the *New York Weekly Journal*, the city's second weekly. Its first issue appeared on 5 November[19]; Zenger's arrest and imprisonment came after another fifty-three editions, on 17 November 1734.

II
Reinventing Journalism
Zenger's Writers and the
First News Events

The events that led up to Zenger's arrest and its historic aftermath were hardly heroic in their original intent but certainly showed a strong measure of journalistic inventiveness and set a sturdy example of the finest tradition of journalism — never to betray a source. The century-old *Appleton's Cyclopedia of American Biography* states that Zenger's *Journal* "... abounded in lampoons and pasquinades[1] that attracted wide attention, and attacked the government with severity, contributing greatly toward loosening the bonds between England and the colonies." But that was only part of the unique approach to American journalism brought by Zenger and his backers.

As the New World's only avowedly partisan news medium, the *New York Weekly Journal* was the predecessor to scores of partisan *Democrats*, *Republicans*, and *Liberals* that were to spring up in the American hinterlands over the next two centuries. This is not meant to imply that the then existing newspapers were impartial or that their publishers had no friends or causes to promote, nor, because of the comparison with more openly partisan papers, that numerous *Times*, *Tribunes*, and *Plain Dealers* have since avoided news policies. Zenger was merely the first American publisher to be candid about his opposition to the prevailing establishment.

Censorship of news is a time-honored tradition of journalists, though very few like to use such a distasteful word in describing their news policies. Sometimes this "censorship" is benign, as in the unanimous reluctance of news media throughout the world to portray Franklin Roosevelt as the severely handicapped cripple that he was during his years as governor of New York and president of the United States. There was a gentlemanly understanding among all members of the

Washington and foreign press corps that this reporting simply wasn't to be done. As a more positive example, by unspoken but industry-wide practice, until recent years the commercial radio and television broadcasters of America always and unanimously gave "front page" treatment to the president of the United States — discarding all other offerings — whenever he felt the public interest called for it. In a number of other cases, the owners of various media have established an individual policy or acquiesced in a collective one to deliver *All the News That's Fit to Print* or to be guided by some similarly catchy but limiting phrase.

In most cases, however, it is the personal judgment of tens of thousands of individual reporters that is the most significant censoring factor in the creation and publication or broadcast of the news. They all come to the scene of any event with their own perspectives and backgrounds (which sometimes become "biases" in the minds of others). They also report or show only what they believe is important. Journalists of Zenger's day were at heart no different from their counterparts of ten generations later.

This voluntary restraint, or gentlemanly courtesy, regarding the presidency of the United States has become submerged in more recent years, due in the greatest part to the fact that journalists of all stripes and persuasions have one trait in common — they dislike being duped or "used." While the peccadilloes of John F. Kennedy in his years as president were known to a number of journalists, they were not considered matters of press corps interest because they did not affect the journalists' confidence in Kennedy's ability to do his job in a creditable manner. That attitude changed abruptly with the Watergate scandal, during which it became clear that Richard Nixon had attempted to deceive the nation's press and through them the people to whom the journalists felt a professional obligation to relay the truth as best they could determine it. With that sea change in standards of taste among the primary source of American political reportage, the mores of journalists everywhere changed in regard to lesser public and even many nonpublic figures.

The coloration of the American political scene in 1734 may have differed in significant details from that of later years — the media of today have undoubtedly become more sophisticated, varied and immediate in their methods of delivery. But the English language is still used in pretty much the same manner, and neither fundamental human nature nor human methods of interpersonal manipulation have undergone significant alteration or improvement.

Isaiah Thomas,[2] America's leading printer and publisher in the Revolutionary period, wrote that Zenger "appears to have been a scholar, but was not correct in the English language, especially in orthography," perhaps due to his early upbringing in a different language. However, Charles Hildeburn,[3] in his detailed analysis of colonial printers, holds a different view. Referring to Zenger's subsequent loss of his positions with the provincial assemblies, Hildeburn maintains, "Both offices were soon lost, however, owing to his being an indifferent printer and very ignorant of the English language; at least Thomas admits the latter, but says he was 'a good workman and a scholar.' His publications absolutely prove the incorrectness of the first assertion and of the second I have found no evidence."

Whatever the nature or mechanical quality of his own personal work, Zenger's press produced a newspaper of less than eighteen years' longevity but of inestimably long-lasting value and influence, one whose initial content clearly originated from fertile and educated minds. The part of James Alexander, Zenger's principal writer and braintruster in the first years of the *Journal*'s operation is an often ignored factor that is well worth mentioning in any history of the evolution of a free press or a free United States. Alexander (1691–1756) was a native of Scotland, where he had participated in the mismanaged Jacobite rebellion of 1715,[4] after which he wisely emigrated to the colonies. In the New World he became surveyor general of New Jersey and in 1723 was appointed as the colony's attorney general. Alexander was later to participate prominently in the 1754 interprovincial conference on Indian relations, held in Albany, over which James DeLancey presided and at which Benjamin Franklin first pushed his plan for a formal federation of the various colonies. Despite this later prominence in the Crown's colonial administration, he could hardly have been counted among the friends of the Hanoverian rulers of Great Britain. Zenger's other backers were also men of local substance and obvious erudition, though less prominent in colonial politics. But, like all mankind, they also had various axes to grind, making it impossible to abstract this story into a simple tale of one heroic printer versus a greedy and dictatorial satrap.

However, if a satrap were to be sought, one might be found in the person of Governor William Cosby (1690–1736). All contemporary chroniclers seem to agree that when Governor Cosby arrived in New York on 1 August 1732, from a visit home to England after his prior post in the Leeward Islands, he was determined to use this opportunity to enhance his personal fortunes by whatever means were available, and there were several. In an even earlier post, as governor of Minorca (from

William Cosby

which he had been "removed"), he had been accused of various crimes of extortion by members of the native aristocracy — reports of which, unfortunately for him, had reached New York long before he did.

Colonial governors consisted "most often of members of aristocratic families whose personal morals, or whose incompetence, were such that it was impossible to employ them nearer home." Since their takeover of the province of New York from the Dutch, "the maladministration of the English governors had before long united both races in a common indignation. ... Governor William Cosby was a fairly common specimen of this representation of the English gentry. He was dull, and had no charm of manner, nor attraction of personal character. He was mean spirited, a little military training had only taught him an affection for petty tyranny, and he was spiteful. He regarded himself as having been sent to New York with permission, legally or illegally, to extort money for himself, so long as he did it quietly."[5]

The simplest of Cosby's enrichment schemes was by the traditional manipulation of official appointments. While the jobs involved were not all that lucrative in terms of salary, they were prestigious and carried opportunities for dabbling lucratively in land deals and other speculations. In the course of abetting his hangers-on, the new governor's flagrant disregard for various influential incumbents, and for the process of public opinion in general, cost him dearly in terms of popular approval and led to a much more organized opposition than he had anticipated. Nevertheless, Cosby continued to use every opportunity available, even appointing his underage son, Billy, to the sinecure post of secretary of the province of New Jersey. After seventeen months on the job, Cosby was granted 22,000 acres in upstate New York, an area then called "Cosby's Manor," better known today as the city of Utica.

Corruption among the royally appointed governors was hardly a new item in the American colonies. In fact, very few of the men assigned to these positions were viewed favorably at that time or in the light of historical hindsight — Robert Hunter of New York and New Jersey being among the exceptions. Cosby was obviously not much different from the lot; they were all basically ignorant of the customs and spirit of those under their administration.[6] But Cosby had the additional misfortune of holding his appointment at a time when those who disagreed with him were better organized and considerably more clever at manipulating public opinion than he.

The somewhat irrelevant spark that set this opposition aflame was the question of what salary was due to the man who had been acting governor for more than a year prior to Cosby's arrival. By tradition, in the absence of a royal appointee, the senior member of the provincial council held gubernatorial authority and was entitled to half the governor's salary — the absent official retaining the rest. However, Rip Van Dam (1660–1749), the man in question, who was a popular shipowner, influential man of substance, and councilor since 1702, decided to test the new arrival's fortitude and refused to part with the new governor's portion unless Cosby gave him an appropriate share of the perquisites that had devolved upon him in England after his appointment but prior to his arrival in New York. Much to the governor's shock, Van Dam's arithmetic showed that the difference between Van Dam's official take in the pertinent period and his own had him owing Van Dam more than £4,431.

The salaries of royal governors in this period were established in London at £1,000 per annum. However, this sum was to be paid by the colonists themselves through local taxation. In most cases the full amount was readily voted by the pertinent legislature, but not always. For instance, in routinely truculent Massachusetts some twenty years earlier, Governor Samuel Shute had found that the General Court had appropriated only £350 as a means of expressing its differences with him on numerous topics. (Cosby seems to have had a somewhat better rapport with the twenty-seven-member New York Assembly than Shute had had with the Massachusetts General Court and was always paid his full salary.)

Frustrated at not getting a favorable settlement from Van Dam voluntarily, Cosby turned to the provincial courts — whose principal functionaries were all within his patronage purview. However, here he had an additional problem. If he brought an action under the common law, the case would have to come before a jury of local folk, most of whom he felt might well be sympathetic to Van Dam. An alternative was to sue in the Court of Chancery, but in the province of New York, the governor was the chancellor and even the most poorly informed royal governor knew better than to hope he could get away with first bringing and then sitting in judgment on his own lawsuit.

Neither of the above being acceptable, Governor Cosby set out to revive a Court of Exchequer by asking the provincial Supreme Court to sit as such. This, too, was a politically risky operation because most colonials distrusted these "equity jurisdictions" which relied on the unelected judges' abstract concepts of justice — not precedent — and, most importantly, sat without juries. Nevertheless, being the least noxious and most dependable of the distasteful remedies open to him, Cosby opted for it. He also arranged for some sailors to swear to an affidavit that Van Dam had fled the Province — "*Non Est Inventus.*" As a fugitive from justice, all his property was then subject to confiscation. Next he ordered his attorney general to enter suit against Van Dam and, late in 1732, arranged for his hand-picked Council to establish a Court of Exchequer in New York.

The following April, the three judges of the provincial Supreme Court sat to hear the case. But Van Dam's lawyers, Messrs. James Alexander and William Smith, immediately argued against the propriety of this sort of court session. William Smith (1697–1768), an English-born graduate of Yale, had arrived in New York in 1715. He was

Rip Van Dam

obviously a scholar, compiling a history of the province to the year 1733, and was to remain prominent in local affairs until his death. An incorporator of Princeton College in 1746, he was also a delegate to the Albany Conference of 1754, where he was elected to the committee "to prepare and receive plans and schemes for the Union of the Colonies."[7] After the dust settled on the Van Dam and Zenger issues, he was appointed provincial attorney general, to the Council in 1752 and to the Supreme Court in 1763.

The chief justice, Lewis Morris, agreed with the position advance by Alexander and Smith, and spoke forcefully on the matter. However, the two associates on the bench, James DeLancey and Frederick Philipse voted in support of the governor. When Cosby heard of Morris' position, he was outraged and demanded a written explanation. Morris, his back now to the wall, was nevertheless quick to oblige him, but went one step further and had *Zenger's Journal* print his response for all to read. At this, Governor Cosby, in the words of a later age "went ballistic" and promptly fired Morris from the court, simultaneously elevating DeLancey to the chief justiceship, a post he would retain for the rest of his life.

Cosby's successive altercations with Van Dam and Morris would precipitate the Zenger controversy. As that controversy brewed, the Van Dam dispute continued, and, ultimately, Cosby would fare as poorly with Van Dam as with Zenger. The former case was weak to start with, and the affidavit of the sailors lost its effectiveness when they could not be found to be questioned further. The case was adjourned repeatedly. In the end, with the fortuitous death of Cosby, the salary matter became moot, and, in any event, the case had already been dropped. With the much greater significance of Zenger's trial, Van Dam's case, which had been at the root of everything, disappeared into the murk of lesser events.

The dissenting judges in the Van Dam hearing, Delancey and Philipse, were to figure prominently in Zenger's subsequent trial. James DeLancey (1703–1760) was a young, native New Yorker of Huguenot ancestry. He had been educated in England, but had returned home and been admitted to the New York bar in 1725. A staunch royalist (his son would be even more so), he not only served as chief justice for the province, but occasionally as acting governor. Frederick Philipse (1695–1751) was the scion of a Dutch colonial family with extensive land holdings. His grandfather, also Frederick, had emigrated from Friesland in 1647 and had acquired a fortune in the Madagascar and slave trades. He was connected, by birth or marriage, with many of the English "establishment" figures of the era.

For his part, Lewis Morris (1671–1746), though stated to be of "Hollander" ancestry, was actually of Welsh descent. An orphan child, brought up by his uncle, he became the first lord of Morrisania, a part of the large tract that had been acquired from Indians by Jonas Bronck and which became part of the city of New York in 1783.[8] By 1730 Morris was already well known as a strenuous opponent of unscrupulous royal appointees — such as Cosby — but had served on the New York Supreme Court since 1715 and on the Council for eight years after 1721. His already dim view of certain royal appointees had been exacerbated by the real estate manipulations of Cosby's "bag man," Harison, which had jeopardized some of Morris' own holdings in Westchester County. Ironically, Morris himself was later (in 1738) appointed the royal governor of New Jersey. His grandsons, Lewis III and Gouverneur, became distinguished figures in the evolution of American freedom and the United States.

Cosby's insult to Morris, while understandable, was severe and prestige-wrecking — not only had Morris held that office for eighteen years, but the chief justiceship was extremely important for the whole Morris clan. Though the family was held in high regard, with the advent (in 1728) of Cosby's predecessor, Governor Montgomerie,[9] they had begun to be eased out of a number of public offices in favor of members of the Philipse family. At this point, the chief justiceship was all they had left; having lost that, there was little alternative for them but to "go to the mat." As a result, Lewis Morris and numerous other highly placed and influential citizens of the province suddenly found themselves allied with Van Dam and his coterie in a vigorous and well-financed "anti–Cosby" faction.

The group made two moves. The first was to set up an opposition medium of expression, for which, in those days, they needed a congenial and reliable printer. Enter John Peter Zenger and the *New York Weekly Journal*, printed on a second-hand press from well-worn pica type, with a subscription price of three shillings per quarter.[10] The group's second and almost coincidental move was to go into politics via the electoral process and seek protected offices in the provincial assembly. As a result, among several other candidatures, both Lewis Morris and his son, Lewis, Jr., ran for the assembly in the elections held in the fall of 1733 and were elected by an overwhelming margin.

In its opening edition, Zenger's *Journal* covered the first of these elections, that of the senior Morris, which took place on the green outside the square structure of St. Paul's Church[11] in Eastchester, on 29 October 1733. The situation made for good reportage. Its reporter being obviously of considerable competence as a writer, Zenger's newspaper covered the event with barely restrained glee and took the opportunity for a number of telling digs at the governor and his cronies:

> On this day Lewis Morris, late Chief Justice of this Province, was by a great majority of voices elected a Representative for the County of Westchester.
>
> This being an election of great expectation, and wherein the court and country's interest was exerted (as is said) to the utmost, I shall give my readers a particular account of it as I had it from a person that was present at it.

Nicholas Cooper,[12] high sheriff of the said county, having by papers affixed to the church of Eastchester and other public places given notice of the day and place of election, without mentioning any time of the day when it was to be done, made the electors on the side of the late judge very suspicious that some fraud was intended; to prevent which about fifty of them kept watch upon and about the green at Eastchester (the place of election) from 12 o'clock the night before until the morning of that day.

The other electors beginning to move on Sunday afternoon and evening so as to be at New Rochelle by midnight, their way lay through Harrison's Purchase, the inhabitants of which provided for their entertainment as they passed, each house in their way having a table plentifully covered for that purpose. About midnight they all met at the house of William Lecount in New Rochelle, whose house not being large enough to entertain so great a number, a large fire was made in the street, by which they sat until daylight, at which time they began to move. They were joined on the hill at the east end of the town by about seventy horse of the electors of the lower part of the county, and then proceeded towards the place of election in the following order.

First rode two trumpeters and three violins; next four of the principal freeholders, one of whom carried a banner on one side of which was affixed in gold capitals KING GEORGE, and on the other, in like golden capitals, LIBERTY AND LAW; next followed the candidate, Lewis Morris, late Chief Justice of this Province; then two colors; and at sunrise they entered upon the green of Eastchester, the place of the election, followed by about three hundred horse of the principal freeholders of the county (a greater number than had ever appeared for one man since the settlement of that county).

About eleven of the clock appeared the candidate of the other side, William Forster, schoolmaster, appointed by the Society for Propagation of the Gospel, and lately made by commission from His Excellency (the present Governor) Clerk of the Peace and Common Pleas in that county; which commission it is said he purchased for the valuable consideration of one hundred pistoles given the Governor.[13] Next to him came two ensigns borne by two of the freeholders; then followed the Honorable James Delancey, Chief Justice of the Province of New York, and the Honorable Frederick Philipse, second judge of the said Province and Baron of the Exchequer, attended by about one hundred seventy horse of the freeholders and friends of the said Forster. The two judges entered the green on the east side, and as they rode twice around it their greeting was "No land tax!" as they passed. The second judge very civilly saluted the late Chief Justice by taking off his hat, which the late judge returned in the same manner.

About an hour after the high sheriff came to town finely mounted, the housings and holster caps being scarlet richly laced with silver…. Upon his approach the electors on both sides went into the green where they were to elect; and after having read His Majesty's writ he bade the electors to proceed to the choice, which they did. A great majority appeared for Mr. Morris, upon which a poll was demanded, but by whom is not known to the relator, though it was said by many to be done by the sheriff himself. Morris, the candidate, several times asked the sheriff upon whose side the majority appeared, but could get no other reply but that a poll must be had.

Accordingly, after about two hours' delay in getting benches, chairs, and tables, they began to poll. Soon after one of those called Quakers, a man of known worth and estate, came to give his vote for the late judge. Upon this Forster and the two Fowlers, Moses and William, chosen by him to be inspectors, questioned his having an estate, and required of the sheriff to tender him the Book to swear in due form of law; which he refused to do, but offered to take his solemn affirmation, which by both the laws of England and the laws of this Province was indulged to the people called Quakers, and had always been practiced from the first election of Representatives in this Province to this time, and never refused. But the sheriff was deaf to all that could be alleged on that side; and notwithstanding that he was told by both the late Chief Justice and James Alexander, one of His Majesty's Council and counsellor-at-law, and by William Smith, counsellor-at-law, that such a procedure was contrary to law and a violent attempt on the liberties of the people, he still persisted in refusing the said Quaker to vote; and in like manner did refuse seven and thirty Quakers more, men of known and visible estates.

About eleven o'clock that night the poll was closed, and it stood thus:

For the late Chief Justice	231
Quakers	38
In all	269

For William Forster	151
The difference	118
	269

So that the late Chief Justice carried it by a great majority without the Quakers.

The indentures being sealed, the whole body of electors waited

on their new Representative to his lodgings with trumpets sounding and violins playing; and in a little time took their leave of him. Thus ended the Westchester election, to the general satisfaction.
    New York, November 5.
    On Wednesday the 31st of October the late Chief Justice, but new Representative for the County of Westchester, landed in this city about five o'clock in the evening at the ferry stairs. On his landing he was saluted by a general fire of the guns from the merchant vessels lying in the road; and was received by great numbers of the most considerable merchants and inhabitants of this city, and by them, with loud acclamations of the people as he walked the streets, conducted to the Black Horse Tavern, where a handsome entertainment was prepared for him at the charge of the gentlemen who received him. In the middle of one side of the room was fixed a tabulet[14] with golden capitals, KING GEORGE, LIBERTY AND LAW.[15]

The Black Horse Tavern was at the corner of South and Garden Streets (now William and Exchange Place) and owned by John DeHoneur. This tavern was a regular meeting place for many groups, largely those in opposition to the royal establishment (which held its gatherings at "Mr. Todd's house," some two blocks away). The New York Assembly's Committee on Grievances met here every Thursday evening, and the younger Pachelbel performed here on 21 January 1736. As the most popular local eatery of that day, it was the site of many celebrations and dinners, of which one of the greatest occurred twenty-two months later, when Zenger's attorney was honored there at a public reception, to be more fully described later in this history.

III
The Evolution of Free Speech
Free Speech from Socrates to 1734

Zenger's actions, trial and vindication collectively form a landmark in the pursuit of personal liberty of conscience and communication and should be recognized for what they represent in the evolution of democracy. In much later years, many elaborate distinctions have been made in the United States and elsewhere between the various mediums of public communication. But the fundamental concept is identical whether one shouts one's message from a soapbox in the city square, nails a broadside to the church door or uses a laser printer, E-mail or various Hertzian waves.

The ancients of Athens and Rome, predecessors of Western civilization, allowed for robust debate in political matters, but this tolerance was not readily arrived at, nor was it without countless exceptions, only the most prominent of which are commonly known two millennia later.[1] In 399 B.C., Socrates was forced to commit suicide for his "impious" transgressions against the Athenian "establishment" — teaching their youth to think for themselves, to question the quality of their form of government and even to not accept the existence of the traditional gods without reservation. Marcus Tullius Cicero (106–43 B.C.) spoke frequently about his concepts of *libertas*, but was finally executed for speaking openly against his long-time political adversary, the triumvir Marcus Antonius. Publius Ovidius Naso (42 B.C.–17 A.D.) got off a little better; he was merely "relegated" to Tomis on the Black Sea after drawing disparaging — if accurate — inferences about the emperor Augustus (and perhaps making a bit too free with the emperor's daughter).

The freedom of speech enjoyed by Romans, though even then centuries old, always remained legally selective. The process started one day in the year 494 B.C. with the ancient equivalent of a general strike, known to history as the "Secession of the Plebs." On that eventful day, the populace (the plebeians) camped en masse on the Aventine Hill and announced that there would be no more work performed until it was given the right to elect spokesmen and a few officials of its own. The ruling patricians were thus coerced into granting a significant measure of status to the aediles and tribunes as representatives of the taxpaying public, as well as into giving an absolute assurance that these representatives would be forever inviolate. This last provision was of the utmost significance and was to reappear as a protection for members of the English Parliament two millennia later in the English Bill of Rights.

In the later years of the empire, when some of these concessions had lapsed (though women maintained — and frequently exercised — the right to divorce their husbands and own property) woe betide even the senator who spoke unfavorably of the emperor's actions and personal habits.

In more modern times, many of the freedoms enjoyed in the Western world (though not that of speech) find their first written assurance in England's Magna Carta, written in 1215 and reluctantly endorsed on the "meadow which is called Runnymede between Windsor and Staines" by a sorely straitened King John, only one year before his death. While the English barons and bishops who caught their liege in a time of economic and religious stringency were much less interested in the rights of the common man than in their own privileges, they did get into writing a few far-reaching concessions from their king that trickled down to all persons with the passage of time.

One should bear in mind that the bulk of this historic document, written in the ecclesiastical Latin of King John's day, deals — often in specific detail — with several of the contemporary grievances that provoked the outrage which put the king into his economic and political straightjacket. Few absolute rulers have ever willingly given much freedom to their subjects[2] but the interdict[3] laid on the English kingdom by Pope Innocent III had brought enormous pressure to bear on the king, for it denied the sacraments and possibly all hope of eternal salvation to his subjects. The purpose of the interdict was not to support the barons; their grievances were a side issue to the pope, whose primary concern was to have John knuckle under to his choice of Stephen Langton as Archbishop of Canterbury. Nevertheless, the English clergy and barons combined nicely in their effort to wring a few concessions from the king, as witnessed by John's salutation:

JOHN, by the grace of God, king of England, lord of Ireland, duke of Normandy and Aquitaine, and count of Anjou, to the archbishops, bishops, abbots, earls, barons, justiciars, foresters, sheriffs, stewards, servants, and to all his bailiffs and faithful subjects, GREETING. Know that we, out of reverence for God and for the salvation of our soul and those of our ancestors and heirs, for the honour of God and the Exaltation of Holy Church, and for the reform of our realm, on the advice of our venerable fathers, Stephen, archbishop of Canterbury, primate of all England and cardinal of the holy Roman church, Henry, archbishop of Dublin, William of London, Peter of Winchester, Jocelyn of Bath and Glastonbury, Hugh of Lincoln, Walter of Worcester, William of Coventry and Benedict of Rochester, bishops, of master Pandulf, subdeacon and member of the household of the Lord Pope, of brother Aymeric, master of the order of Knights Templar in England, and of the noble men William Marshal earl of Pembroke, William earl of Salisbury, William earl of Warenne, William earl of Arundel, Alan of Galloway constable of Scotland, Warin fitz Gerold, Peter fitz Herbert, Hubert de Burgh seneschal of Poitou, Hugh de Neville, Matthew fitz Herbert, Thomas Basset, Alan Basset, Philip de Aubeney, Robert of Ropsley, John Marshal, John fitz Hugh, and others, our faithful subjects:

The recitation of so many churchmen in its preamble shows how serious was the impact of the pope's interdict. Nevertheless, despite having their king "on the ropes" the barons and bishops let John get away with a few face-saving phrases scattered throughout the rest of the document. Fortunately, this liberality did little to lessen the fundamental significance of the royal concessions. Here follow a few of the more relevant and enduring clauses among the sixty-three that followed and which have their modern expression in the basic "law of our land."

(1) In the first place we have granted to God, and by this our present Charter confirmed for us and our heirs for ever that the English Church shall be free, and shall have its rights undiminished and its liberties unimpaired; and it is our will that it be thus observed; which is evident from the fact that, before the quarrel between us and our barons began, we willingly and spontaneously granted and by our charter confirmed the freedom of elections which is reckoned most important and very essential to the English Church, and obtained confirmation of it from the lord pope Innocent III; the which we will observe and we wish our heirs to observe it in good faith forever. We have also granted to all free men of our kingdom,

for ourselves and out heirs for ever, all the liberties written below, to be had and held by them and their heirs of us and our heirs.

(17) Common pleas shall not follow our court, but shall be held in some fixed place. [As pointedly noted in the American Declaration of Independence, the ministers of King George III obviously had a lapse of memory on this point.]

(18) Recognitions of novel disseisin,[4] of mort d'ancester,[5] and of darrein presentment,[6] shall not be held elsewhere than in the counties to which they relate, and in this manner — we, or if we should be out of the realm, our chief justiciar, will send two justices through each county four times a year, who with four knights of each county chosen by the county, shall hold the said assizes in the county and on a day and in the place of meeting of the county court.

(20) A free man shall not be amerced[7] for a trivial offense except in accordance with the degree of the offense, and for a grave offense he shall be amerced in accordance with its gravity, yet saving his way of living; and a merchant in the same way, saving his means of livelihood — if they have fallen into our mercy; and none of the aforesaid amercements shall be imposed except by the oath of good men of the neighborhood. [This concept is encompassed in Amendment VIII to the U.S. Constitution.]

(28) No constable or other bailiff of ours shall take anyone's corn or other chattels unless he pays on the spot in cash for them or can delay payment by arrangement with the seller.

(30) No sheriff, or bailiff of ours, or anyone else shall take the horses or carts of any free man for transport work save with the agreement of that freeman.

(31) Neither we nor our bailiffs will take, for castles or other works of ours, timber which is not ours, except with the agreement of him whose timber it is.

(38) No bailiff shall in future put anyone to trial upon his own bare word, without reliable witnesses produced for this purpose.

(39) No free man shall be arrested or imprisoned or disseized[8] or outlawed or exiled or in any way victimized, neither will we attack him or send anyone to attack him, except by the lawful judgement of his peers or by the law of the land. [This was a significant but subsidiary issue in the Zenger trial.]

(40) To no one will we sell, to no one will we refuse or delay right or justice.

The most important of these ancient and traditional English liberties can be found, reworded after the passage of almost six centuries to fit a later context, in the American Bill of Rights.

However, and presaging a further and more famous misunderstanding between the English and the Papacy, when Pope Innocent III heard of the Magna Carta, he officially and formally "disallowed" it. This ecclesiastical procedure had minimal political impact on the English barons, and not much on the prelates either. But, almost immediately upon the death of King John a backsliding trend set in. The barons went along for a while under the regency during the childhood of Henry III, but by 1236 they felt he was mature enough to need a reminder. They assembled in force at Merton, just outside London, to emphasize the point.

When Henry came into his own, such as it was, he continued to ignore as much of the great charter as he could, thereby keeping his barons in a state of incipient insurrection for most of his long reign. In 1258 they assembled again at Oxford and publicly adopted a number of "provisions" further restricting the king's powers. But in 1261, Henry, who has not been treated much better by historians than by his contemporaries, managed to get Pope Innocent IV to "disallow" the Oxford Provisions, too. However, by then the idea of having a Privy Council to "advise and consent" on the king's appointments was in place to stay.

Very soon after William Caxton's printing press was set up in England in 1476, it was realized that this device possessed great usefulness in the dissemination of information and, beyond that, in influencing the minds of men. Rulers, however, have always questioned the merit in making too much information available to their subordinates for fear of what disrespectful thoughts might thus be engendered. Giving credit to the hazards of excessive communication, Otto von Bismarck, the ultimate political realist, made the wry observation, some years later, that "[C]redence cannot be placed in the truth of any report until it has been officially denied."

Indeed, some scholars have related the evolution of printing with the rise of modern democracy. By the same token, as presses became more available, it was the risks of open, mass communication that led various royal authorities to try bringing them under some sort of official control. These efforts reached a high point in 1586 when Queen Elizabeth's Star Chamber decreed that all books must be reviewed *prior to publication* by either the Archbishop of Canterbury or the Archbishop of London. This procedure — but not the basic concept — was amended in 1641 by the Puritan parliament, which also eliminated King Charles I and the Star Chamber. But the revised measure continued to be evaded as often as observed.

A Board of Licensors was established in 1643 in a continuing effort to prohibit the publication of questionable or offensive material. This was followed, in 1662, after the restoration of King Charles II, by a Licensing of Printing Act that was only occasionally effective — for example, in 1663 when Thomas Brewster was convicted for printing a tract that defended those who had been party to the execution of Charles I. However, "bootleg" printing continued to exasperate the monarch throughout his reign. In mid–December 1684, Charles II gave power to one of his surrogates to search and seize papers and presses so as to "stop these intolerable liberties of the press." Finally, after the deposition of James II in 1688 and the accession of more appealing sovereigns to the throne in 1689, the entire process of trying to keep a lid on this form of human communication was scrapped. In 1694, the Licensing Act was allowed to lapse without renewal, five years after the English Bill of Rights was adopted.

The first half of the Bill of Rights — an "Act Declaring the Rights and Liberties of the Subject and Settling the Succession of the Crown" — clarified some of the already traditional English liberties, which King James II was charged with violating. Most specifically, it was stated that the recently evicted monarch had dispensed with the law in numerous cases, levied taxes and maintained a standing army without the consent of parliament.[9] By virtue of the 1689 act all future English kings were henceforth required to give members of Parliament the same protection as Roman patricians did the tribunes after the Aventine uprising. These elected representatives were also assured of complete freedom of speech while acting as such. In stating the succession to the throne, however, this act made it abundantly clear that any one who "shall profess the popish religion, or marry a papist, shall be excluded and be for ever incapable to inherit, possess or enjoy the crown and government of this realm."[10]

Some historians have credited Thomas Gordon (d. 1750) with making the most effective use of the newly achieved, if still poorly accepted, right to publish freely and thus to enhance other related rights. An obviously well educated Scot (from Kirkudbright), he was admitted to the bar in 1716 and then migrated to London, where he came to the attention of the Whig politician, John Trenchard,[11] with whom he found great compatibility. Collectively the pair became pamphleteers on numerous topics, but became best known for their collaboration after 1720 on a series of essays labeled *Cato's Letters*.

They picked a good name and one that has continued to be used among those wishing to evoke nobility of purpose in their work. Marcus Portius Cato (95–45 B.C.), called "The Younger" to distinguish him from his father, "The Censor," was notable for his vigorous personal integrity, his opposition to the imperial ambitions of Julius Caesar and his devotion to the Roman Republic. His death was by suicide after Caesar came to absolute power.

First published in the *London Journal*, they were combined and reprinted as a four-volume set after Trenchard's death in 1723. But *Cato's Letters* would enjoy an even wider circulation, some of them being reprinted as far away as in the colonies. In addition to his own "Silence Dogood" letters in 1722, Benjamin Franklin printed excerpts from "Cato's" fifteenth essay, on the topic of freedom of speech: "[It] is the great Bulwark of Liberty; they prosper and die together."[12] Franklin had been driven to this emphatic defense of free speech when the Massachusetts General Court imprisoned his employer and older brother, James, for having ridiculed the effectiveness of the Bay colony government's attempts at suppression of piracy in his weekly paper, *New England Courant.*[13] In "Cato's" far-sighted and eloquent words, "[W]ithout Freedom of thought, there can be no such Thing as Wisdom; and no such Thing as publick Liberty, without Freedom of Speech; Which is the Right of every Man, as far as by it he does not hurt and control the Right of another; and this is the only check which it ought to suffer, the only bounds which it ought to know."

In his thirty-second essay, "Cato" laid the intellectual foundation for Zenger's acquittal a dozen years later: "A Libel is not the less a Libel for being true. This may seem a contradiction, but it is neither one in Law, or in common Sense. There are some Truths not fit to be told; where for Example, the Discovery of a small Fault may do great Mischief: or the Discovery of a great Fault can do no Good, there ought to be no Discovery at all; and to make Faults where there are none, is still worse. But this doctrine only holds true as to private and personal Failings; and it is quite otherwise when the Crimes of Men come to affect the Publick. The exposing of publick Wickedness, as it is a Duty which every Man owes to the Truth and his Country, are never to be a Libel in the Nature of Things."

Gordon's liberal tendencies combined fruitfully with his classical education in the publication of numerous other pamphlets over the ensuing years following *Cato's Letters.* These included, in 1744, "The Works of Sallust with Political Discourses upon That Writer" and an edition of Cicero's "Four Orations Against Catiline." Three years later he produced an "Essay on Government." However, Gordon's polemic vigor may well have declined in his later years after the first Whig prime minister, Sir Robert Walpole (1676–1745), put him on the government payroll as Great Britain's first "commissioner of wine licenses," an office which one anonymous observer stated "much diminished his patriotism."

The awakening philosophy of human rights was already giving thoughtful men the courage to stand up in defense of principle. But, as the elder Franklin discovered in 1722, as well as Zenger a dozen years later and many another crusading journalist and truth seeker in the centuries before and after, one seldom wins friends in high places when one publishes unwelcome truth. Invariably the effect is quite the opposite. But after Zenger's trial and acquittal, juries across America almost invariably refused to convict journalists who were critics of government — as long as their defense was based on truth.

While Gordon exploited the new printing technology, a massive groundswell of political thinking was coming over much of the Western world. The "divine right" of absolute monarchy, among the other dogmas, was under critical scrutiny. And when looked at closely, royalty's divinity — like the emperor's new clothing — was invisible. With a few bumpy episodes, this trend towards popular sovereignty, begun in 1215 and expanded in 1689, continued, being forcefully articulated in the American Declaration of Independence, restated in the French Declaration of the Rights of Man and of the Citizen, and crossing the Atlantic again to appear in the first ten amendments to the United States Constitution.

It is an interesting anomaly that the basic principles of a government founded on the "consent of the governed" were worked out largely in secret. During that summer of 1787, while the delegates of Rhode Island stayed home, the other fifty-five men kept their arguments behind closed doors — and even swore their official printers (Dunlap and Claypoole) to secrecy. Having concluded their work, however, they were so proud of it that almost every — all eighty-odd — newspaper in the new nation printed the resulting document in full, many of them running second editions. By so doing they gave an element of justification to Jefferson's often quoted opinion that, given the option, he would prefer newspapers without government to government without newspapers.

It may also be more than coincidental that the final wording of the United States Constitution was entrusted to a committee headed by Gouverneur Morris, who eliminated a recitation of various states and individuals in his preamble, an act which won immediate acclaim and showed clearly how far the groundswell had gone towards making the governed the ultimate jury: "*We the People* of the United States, in Order to form a more perfect Union, Establish Justice, insure domestic Tranquility...."

The more realistic analyst of human affairs encountering the concept of truth in matters relating to government should note that things may not have changed a great deal despite a number of supposedly good intentions and the passage of two and a half centuries. Governments and their functionaries have never been noted for consistent devotion to candor. This virtue is not mandated by the Ten Commandments nor is it mentioned anywhere in the United States Constitution. In war it is, as Senator Hiram Johnson ruefully noted in 1917, "the first casualty," and he might well have expanded his comment to include a number of other fields of human endeavor.

Modern-day Americans continually rediscover the never-ending issue of "truth in politics," trying to require "on the job" performance from those elected to public office after having inspired voter support by pledges ranging from "two cars in every garage" to "read my lips." However, the failure of public officials to live up to expectations is generally taken by most sophisticated voters with the same credibility applied to used car salesmen. On balance, in these matters the people seem to have gotten pretty much what they deserved. More severe are the massive and deliberate deceptions that have not infrequently been perpetrated on the people of all nations by their leaders in the name of national security—especially during times of war.

Equally alarming, these policies of misinformation have almost always received a good measure of support from the news media, either by virtue of imposed censorship or from journalistic complacency and cowardice. Far worse in their ultimate impact than the relatively minor peccadilloes of royal governors such as Cosby, such deceptions have had a number of far reaching consequences. A few examples from modern history will illustrate the point.

With the complicity of Britain's leading newspaper, *The Times*, the British public was never informed of the nation's disgracefully incompetent military leadership and ill-preparedness during the Crimean War. Though this did maintain civilian support, it also massaged the British people into a complacency about the military's command system that persisted into the slaughterous practices of World War I.

From the Verdun offensive in 1916 on, the German people were never told the enormity of the nation's casualties. This deception fostered the wholly false impression in the minds of the German people that they had been "betrayed" by their leaders *after* the Armistice, rather than before, thus leading to the rise of Hitler. At the same time, the French poilus were being equally poorly served by the persistent use of theoretical and wholly unrealistic enemy casualty estimates to make it appear the Germans were suffering even worse losses than they were and that the de Grandmaison philosophy of *l'attaque à outrance*[14] was effectively winning the war.

In World War II the American government, for mistaken policy reasons, withheld the truth about Chinese Nationalist corruption (as Americans understood the word) and incompetence. Thereby, we alienated the far more effective Chinese "Communists," who took our support of Chiang Kai-shek as an American endorsement of their mortal enemies. Twenty years later, America again failed in an Asian war, which our government (throughout four different administrations) kept insisting we were winning. The suppression of truth not only gulled the public for a while, but caused America's leaders to believe their own lies and thereby to compound their errors in South Vietnam, at terrible cost.

This is not the place to explain the phenomenon of human egos standing in the way of truthfulness. But no realistic person should fail to appreciate that this condition is what lies at the root of a great deal of national misery and public misunderstanding — and that these problems are not new.

IV
The Evolution of Related Freedoms
Thought and Religion

Freedom of thought includes the right to believe — or not believe — in anything, be it of a religious, political, social, economic or any other nature. However, while one can always think what one wishes — and we all do, in the privacy of our hearts — it is the expression of these thoughts that brings on all manner of trouble.

It is difficult and wrong to separate the evolution of individual freedoms between the English-speaking peoples on two sides of the Atlantic Ocean. Despite our occasional differences of opinion, our common cultural and legal heritages remain far too strong and our commerce and literature continually cross-fertilize each with the other. It is also wrong to separate the evolution of some selective human freedoms from the general trend in this direction over several centuries among most segments of human society. However, one fact is clear: in the last two centuries, English personal liberties have profited greatly from the example of their irreverent American cousins, though continuing to lag behind them even to this date.[1]

"Wrong thinkers," however, have been among us forever. With the poor "P.R." that the Church of Rome came to "enjoy" among European intellectuals during the late Middle Ages, the matter of correctness in religious thinking became an enormously divisive issue. It divided families, cities, even whole nations, causing immense, long-lasting acrimony and countless wars. But, as the leading nation in the early evolution of personal freedoms, as we presently understand them, the issue of religious correctness has greater significance when examined in the context of the British Isles.

Problems within the Catholic establishment in England may not

41

have been all that different from those of the Church of Rome elsewhere in the Middle Ages. They were largely self-induced by the Church, for the insistence of a long series of popes to maintain a temporal kingdom of their own in Italy certainly did not enhance a papal image of detachment from secular concerns. Even more problematic in England was the long (and well-documented) record of ecclesiastical laxity in behaving as expected of those attuned more to the hereafter than to the present. The Church, as it operated in England, was run by humans as greedy as any in our species. There would not have been nearly as many ecclesiastical names in the preamble to the Magna Carta of 1215 had not these people already been deeply involved in secular machinations. Only a few years later, Pope Innocent IV felt it necessary to dispatch a special legate, Otto, Cardinal Bishop of Palestrina, to investigate complaints about clerical conduct that had reached his ears in Rome.

Thus it was that Otto arrived in England in late June 1237 and stayed for three-and-a-half years. In December 1237, he convened a council in London, which listed twenty-four abuses as being in need of immediate rectification. Thereafter many of the better English bishops adopted canons for their jurisdictions, only some of which had any lasting effect. In the words of one Oxford lecturer, "The general picture ... [was of] ... a clergy slack, ignorant, backward, unspiritual even when not actually immoral, greedy of fees; often illiterate, gamblers, brawlers, professional false witnesses; in a word, a state of things crying aloud for drastic and continuous action on the part of the central power." [2]

Whether England's final break with the Church of Rome was caused by resentment at the seeming overenrichment of monasteries,[3] or Henry VIII's desire to have a different wife, or the triumph of fallible human nature over sporadic reforming efforts such as that of Otto, the causes became immaterial once the break had occurred. However, as was only to be expected, though the king's friends did all right, the common folk got precious little from the despoliation of the monasteries.[4] The most significant outcome of the king's break with Rome was that the power structure of Great Britain became largely Protestant, and those who adhered to the clerical authority of Rome became outcasts, denigrated and persecuted.

The peoples of northern Europe, England in particular, had a further and somewhat porochial, but understandable reason for seeing little merit in maintaining an adherence to the papacy. Of all the hundreds of popes, only one, Adrian IV (Nicholas Breakspear; d. 1159), was of English birth, and he lasted barely four years on the job. Popes were almost unanimously selected from natives of Latin-language countries;

to the English, papal agents, confidants and appointees were almost unanimously foreign and unacquainted with local interests. Thus they almost always became a common enemy that served to unify the otherwise squabbling barons of Great Britain.

There were other political factors engendering a poor relationship, too. By the fifteenth century, France had become England's traditional opponent; meanwhile, the papacy was increasingly percieved as a French fiefdom.[5] In 1493, Pope Alexander VI (Rodrigo Borgia) arrogantly divided the world between the Spanish and the Portuguese, with neither an ort nor an ait left over for anyone else. Of course, the fact that he admitted to four illegitimate children by a Roman lady (including Cesare and Lucretia) did little to enhance his "odor of sanctity" or papal prestige in general. As time went on, and as events like the Spanish Armada proved, the Church of Rome took on every worldly appearance of being owned and operated by the political and military enemies of England.

All religions tend to be inherently conservative, holding to traditions and rituals that ever fewer participants can relate to current reality. In the Western world this conservatism of thought was at its strongest during the time of the Inquisition, an ill-begotten attempt at purification which followed closely on the great Protestant schism. Examples abound of the non-religious suppressions of indubitable secular fact that were nevertheless denounced as "heresy." Miguel Serveto (1511–1553), a Spanish theologian and physician, though also an opponent of infant baptism, was burned at the stake (with the collaboration of Calvin) for having disputed the views of Galen on pulmonary circulation of the blood. Johannes Baptista van Helmont (1579–1644) was the first to understand the composition of the atmosphere, a point which he proved by planting a willow tree in a container holding two hundred pounds of dirt. Five years later, the tree had gained 169 pounds but the weight of dirt was unchanged. Hated by the Jesuits for his freedom of thought, he was condemned and forced to recant. Galileo Galilei (1564–1642) was "admonished" by the pope in 1616 and later forced to recant his support of the Copernican concept of a heliocentric universe rather than a geocentric one.

As a result of these complications, religious toleration after the mid–sixteenth century remained about as acceptable as any other form of treason. However, in the Western world, where one was susceptible to any shift in the thinking of one's ruler, or shift of the ruler for that matter, it was a vastly greater game of chance to be outspoken on differing views than in the days when all men owed ultimate allegiance to the bishop of Rome and kept any variances in thought carefully to themselves. This intolerance bred not only censorship, to help keep the public's mind pure, but loss of liberty and property without trial for many who were merely believed to hold views contrary to established authority.

As England lurched from mostly Protestant Tudors to semi–Catholic Stuarts to the Cromwellian Protectorate and back again, no one knew exactly what faith to cling to— at least in public. But once free of Rome, the British power structure tended to stay independent, regardless of the momentary persuasion of the incumbent monarch. Thus, even the king, particularly James II (1633–1701), found it difficult to maintain both his Roman faith and his throne. In 1688, after less than four years on the job, he gave up trying and fled the country.[6]

King James II, no liberal in terms of his appointees as royal governors, has taken a bum rap on the question of religion. While he made no secret of his adherence to the Church of Rome, he was equally confirmed in his toleration of other faiths. As Duke of York and overseer of his brother's colonial ventures, James had instructed Governor Edmund Andros[7] in 1672: "You shall permit all persons of what Religion soever, quietly to inhabit within the precincts of your jurisdiction without giving them any disturbance or disquiet whatever for, or by reason of, their differing opinions in matters of Religion; provided they give no disturbance to the public peace, nor do molest or disquiet others in the free exercise of their religion."

King James's devotion to "popery," however, survived his rule and thrived among the progeny of his second marriage — to the very Catholic Mary of Modena. This resulted in countless abortive military attempts (mostly by the Scots) to reinstate Stuart pretenders, one of which (in 1745) came remarkably close to succeeding. James himself, with the half-hearted assistance of Louis XIV, launched only one attempt to regain his throne. That effort ended in Ireland in 1690 with the disastrous Battle of the Boyne. His son, the "Old Pretender," James Francis Edward (1688–1766), and his grandson, the "Young Pretender," known in Scotland as Bonnie Prince Charlie (1720–1788), remained ever true to their "popish" faith and are both buried in St. Peter's in Rome — the one identified as James III and the other as Charles III.

After the "Glorious Revolution" of 1689 saw the arrival of the Protestant Prince William of Orange on the British throne with his Stuart wife, Mary,[8] the Tolerance Act and the English Bill of Rights were adopted, the latter of which came down heavily against "popery" but specified (among other provisions) "that freedom of speech and debate on proceedings in Parliament ought not to be impeached or questioned in any court or place out of parliament." However, for anyone outside of the privileged halls of Parliament to vent an unfavorable opinion of the government was still a "seditious libel" and open to severe punishment.

Though thus protected, Parliament itself—as personified by the House of Commons—was hardly a fair representation of the English populace. The Irish barely counted at all,[9] and some "boroughs" were constituted with only a handful of voters—to keep them "safe"; while others were a thousand times larger. Those "rotten boroughs" were finally corrected by a parliamentary reform act of 1832, by which time 20 percent of the seats in the House were held by members representing less than fifty voters each, among a total population of some 25 million.

The language protective of open parliamentary debate reached across the Atlantic Ocean to find fertile soil in the minds of various educated colonists. At the same time, the New England town meeting, which grew up in the absence of a landed gentry that made decisions, further fostered the idea of public discussion prior to taking any public action, a fundamental building block of democracy. In this fertile environment, protection of open debate became the foundation of the American provision stated in the 1781 Articles of Confederation: "Freedom of speech and debate in Congress shall not be impeached or questioned in any court or place out of Congress."[10]

The Continental Congress was stimulated in its adoption of such language by phrases previously stated by the legislatures of several states. For instance, the 1780 Massachusetts Declaration of Rights (largely drafted by John Adams) called for a similar condition, but pertinent in its case to its own General Court[11]: "freedom of deliberation, speech and debate, in either house of the legislature is so essential to the rights of the people, that it cannot be the foundation of any accusation or prosecution, action or complaint, in any other court or place whatsoever." However, the Virginia Declaration of Rights of 1776 (largely drafted by James Madison) had already gone a bit farther, stating—in words taken from "Cato's" fifteenth essay—that "Freedom of the Press is one of the greatest bulwarks of liberty, and can never be restrained but by despotic governments." And a few years later the emphatic phrase, "Congress shall make no law," came directly from the official report of New Hampshire's legislative convention of 1789, during which it approved the new nation's basic legal system and structure.

As we will see, the arrogance of the royally appointed judges in the Zenger trial, DeLancey and Philipse, who had already been tainted in the popular mind by their positions in the suit against Van Dam, was obviously thoroughly resented by the jury. But this was only one manifestation of a feeling on the part of free men that they were entitled to some say in the judicial process under which they lived. The American Revolution was tindered by these resentments, but sparked into life by the Sugar Act of 1764 and the Stamp Act of 1765, both of which — by relying on Admiralty enforcement procedures — disallowed the colonists their traditional English right to trial by a jury of their peers. This was bad enough, but Parliament also instituted a tax on these (and other) commodities in every colony without giving the residents any say in the matter, thus giving tremendous ammunition to firebrands such as Sam Adams. All these events led up to the common realization (which Benjamin Franklin had been preaching for a decade) that in unity there might lie strength. But with a population of less than 4 million,[12] the colonies would need all the unity they could to face a British nation then numbering some 15 million.[13] It was these impingements on traditional rights, widely reported in the colonial press, that gave rise to the first real expression of colonial unity — the Continental Congress of 1765.

The American Revolution, therefore, was not a case of opposition to British traditions or even British rule, though the abuses inflicted by many royal governors certainly gave ammunition to the firebrands among the colonists. It was, instead, a determined effort by people who felt themselves to be the heirs to as much freedom as was guaranteed in England, who wanted to retain what they believed to be their natural and hereditary rights. All educated people in the colonies knew that both the Magna Carta and English Bill of Rights made it clear their individual rights could not be advanced or withheld at the whim of any king, governor or parliament — whether they had emigrated across the ocean or stayed in their mother country.

Freedom of religion is a companion to freedom of speech and the press — indeed, the assurance of all three rights to the American people is found in the same sentence of the First Amendment. And like freedom of speech and press, freedom of religion was hardly a precondition of life in America. A brutal lack of religious tolerance was such a pervasive hallmark of life in England and Europe in general, well before and long after the beginning of migrations to the New World, that the concept traveled the ocean as intellectual baggage with every arrival during the seventeenth century.

The Puritans who settled the Bay colony after 1620, soon established a state religion that was not fully and legally disestablished from the commonwealth of Massachusetts until 1833. In 1635, before the tentacles of the Bay settlement had reached inland to the Connecticut River and before John Harvard had left his books to a college, Roger Williams and his coterie were banished from the colony's midst to settle among the Indians across the Seekonk River in the Providence Plantations because they would not profess conformance to prevailing dogma as determined by the General Court of Massachusetts.

Farther south, Cecilius Calvert, Lord Baltimore, founded his settlement for Catholics in Maryland, endowing it as an inducement to settlement, with a subsequently well-advertised (if short-lived) freedom of religion that unfortunately only extended to those "professing to believe in Jesus Christ."

Though not as well publicized as Baltimore's toleration, William Penn did better with his settlement for Quakers (who were particularly unpopular among the Puritans); his clause on this topic protected the religious freedom of "all persons who acknowledge God to be the creator of the world." The ostracism of George Keith, however, and the destruction of his writings showed that even the Penns had serious thin spots regarding religious tolerance. And in the 1720s, with the placement of so many Palatine and other German emigrants of Lutheran persuasion in Pennsylvania, the assembly noted that the very loyalty of the colony to the crown was at stake.

To the north, New Hampshire, though occasionally under the political domination of Massachusetts, showed itself to be considerably ahead of its southern neighbors with the enactment of a provision in colonial law for complete religious toleration as early as 1693.

All the while, in England, the Church of England continued (up to the present day) its state-supported position, though the individual ability to worship freely as one pleases was extended to all persons in 1859.

Other societies evolved their individual freedoms more slowly, while a few (like the French in 1789) did so with startling suddenness. In Japan, the "Meije Restoration," resulting from the overthrow of the Tokugawa shogunate in 1867, was led by the youthful and newly installed emperor Mutsuhito, known as Meije Tenno (1852–1912) and brought such a surge of westernization that there was an ongoing series of minor revolts among the peasantry and others. But the germ of intellectual freedom remained firmly planted. It was not, however, until the military occupation by American forces in 1945 and the consequent renunciation of divinity by the Emperor that any citizen could speak or write with total freedom on any topic.

The American Bill of Rights did not arrive unrehearsed from any one mind, such as that of James Madison, as is often believed of the Constitution. However, it is fair to note that Madison's contributions to *The Federalist* over several prior years had come to the attention of most persons active in the political process and had influenced the deliberations of many councils and legislatures. As a sign of considerable progress, the Northwest Ordinance of 1787 — one of the few successful measures carried out under the Articles of Confederation — intended to provide for the governance of the territory of the later states of Ohio, Indiana, Illinois, Michigan and Wisconsin and included several of the protections soon to be covered in the first ten amendments.

Many of the clauses, as noted above, were already in place as state constitutions by the actions of various state (or colonial) legislatures. But more importantly, in their ratification conventions, several states offered specific language the gist of which was combined and incorporated by the Congress in its final draft. Of these suggestions North Carolina and Virginia proposed the most, but Massachusetts, New Hampshire, New York, Maryland and South Carolina added significantly.

Interestingly, two other proposals had been before the Congress but were rejected along the tortuous route to acceptance and thus never made it into the final version of Bill of Rights:

(1) It was believed that the Congress should remain close to the people to prevent its members being so involved with their own personal concerns that they ignored the interests of their constituents. A proposed First Amendment would have maintained a representative-to-population ratio of 1/30,000 until there were 100 members of the lower house, then a ratio of 1/40,000 until there were 200, thereafter a ratio of 1/50,000. Given that ratio, the House of Representatives would, for example, have reached the unwieldy mass of 3,000 during World War II and close to 6,000 at this time of writing.

(2) Under a second proposal the Congress would have been forbidden to vote itself a raise in pay effective before the next election had taken place.

Since Delaware had already rejected such clauses when they were proposed under the Articles of Confederation, the unanimity necessary for their adoption at that time was lacking, and thereafter these ideas failed to ever gain sufficient adherents. In retrospect, the former would probably have proven extremely chaotic, but the latter has always enjoyed strong ethical and political appeal among the public, though hardly as much among the incumbents.

Perhaps the most meaningful, if least appreciated, provision in the Bill of Rights is its last one, which reserves every power and duty not specifically granted to the federal government to those of the various constituent states or — in Gouverneur Morris' phrase — "to the people." While this reservation was in keeping with Morris' theme, it also had an important political motivation since reserving all unspecified rights to the states thus became an assurance of ratification of the new order.

V

Colonial Newspapers

The Early Print Media of America

News media, as they are presently understood, are a relatively late development in human communications. From earliest recorded times, the favorite method of spreading information was clearly by what might be called "gossip." Written material was both costly and rare — paper was not in common supply until the late Middle Ages. Relatively few persons, even those in positions of secular power, could read and write until the early nineteenth century. Written documents were primarily used by those who could not hope to speak personally to all the individuals who would benefit from the information; the writers, moreover, had to rely on a relatively few literate persons to read the resulting document to its full audience. Thus, throughout most of human history, mass communication was primarily by word of mouth — the town crier, the forum, the local assembly. Print media, as we know them presently, only became possible with Guttenberg's invention, and evolved thereafter almost in direct proportion to the increase in human numbers that accompanied the dawn of industrialization — and colonialism.

Throughout all times, however, even to the present day, the fear of giving the governed too much information has afflicted the thought process of the governors. In fundamental fact, neither King George II nor William Cosby was much different from Richard Nixon and his secretive minions.

Newspapers — of a sort — began to appear in England during the early years of the Stuart kings. At first they were weekly affairs, almost always under official license and offering in greatest part news from distant regions. The first presses were mostly located in the capital city of London, and since the royal mail went out from that city on Tuesdays and Saturdays, those became the press dates for the earliest papers.

The first daily paper, appearing under the benign reign of the later Stuarts, was the *London Courant* which began operation on 11 March 1702. Across the Atlantic, the first paper to last beyond its initial issue was a weekly, the *Boston News Letter*, which began operation on 24 March 1704. Being printed under the auspices of John Campbell, postmaster of Boston, it was unlikely to suffer the fate of Harris' *Publick Occurrences*, and in fact it survived for seventy-two years. As a journal it held the further distinction of being the first periodical in America to run an illustration — in its issue of 19 January 1707 — a woodcut of the new flag proposed for the United Kingdom of England and Scotland. When Campbell was replaced as postmaster in 1719, he refused to turn over this interesting sideline to his official successor. The retention must have been caused by a motive other than profit, however, as Campbell complained in a contemporary issue that he could not make a living with a circulation of only three hundred, "tho' some ignorantly concludes he Sells upwards of a Thousand." Weary of it all, in 1722, Campbell retired in favor of his printer, Bartholomew Green.

John Brooker, the successor postmaster, not to be denied in his desire for a paper of his own, brought out a competing entity, the *Boston Gazette*, on 21 December 1719, the second durable news medium in the colonies, which continued as an organ of the postmastership under several of Brooker's successors. It's officially approved status was, however, clear from the start, for its masthead stated in large type: "Published by Authority."

On 7 August 1721, a startling new arrival appeared on the Boston newsstands, the *New England Courant*, fresh from the press of James Franklin. This was another weekly, the third in Boston and the fourth in the colonies. It is better known in the history of journalism, however, as the newspaper at which Benjamin Franklin got his start, with his "Silence Dogood" letters. It is especially notable for being the first newspaper in any of the colonies to be offered in clear opposition to the established authorities. As such, the *Courant*'s proprietors almost immediately encountered a series of tribulations that presaged those of Zenger in New York a dozen years later. In late July 1722, the Massachusetts governor and his council proposed that, prior to James Franklin's release from confinement for his piracy stories, he should be placed under a bond that required prior approval of all subsequent issues before printing.. The Council's proposal was based on its statement that "many Passages have been published, boldly reflecting on His Majesty's Government and on the Administration of it within this

Province, the Ministry, Churches and College [Harvard]: and it very often contains Paragraphs that tend to fill the Readers Minds with vanity, to the Dishonor of God and disservice to Good Men." In this opening skirmish for the cause of journalistic liberty, however, the elected Massachusetts legislature refused to concur with the idea of prior censorship, and Franklin was soon printing further articles that gave offense. So the following January, a joint committee of the Council and legislature reported that:

> The Committee appointed to Consider of the Paper called *The New England Courant*, published Monday ... are humbly of Opinion that the Tendency of said Paper is to mock Religion, and bring it into Contempt, that the Holy Scriptures are therein profanely abused, that the Reverend and faithful Ministers of the Gospel are injuriously Reflected on, His Majesty's Government affronted, and the Peace and good Order of his Majesty's Subjects of the Province disturbed by the said *Courant*; And for the prevention of the like Offense for the Future, the Committee humbly propose, That James Franklin the Printer and Publisher thereof, be strictly forbidden by this Court to Print or Publish the *New England Courant*, or any Pamphlet or Paper of the like Nature, except that it be first supervised by the Secretary of this Province; and the Justices of His Majesty's Sessions of the Peace for the County of Suffolk, at their next Adjournment, be directed to take sufficient Bonds of the said Franklin for [his good behavior] Twelve Months Time.

The immediate cause of the elder Franklin's discomfiture in the Bay colony had been his taking issue with the dictum of Increase Mather and other leading Puritans that inoculation should be used as a means of combating the spread of small pox. In the third issue of Franklin's paper, it was baldly stated as a "chief design" of the paper "to oppose the *doubtful* and *dangerous* Practice of *inoculating* the *Small Pox*." Journalists have been known to be wrong — even if their subsequent admissions of error are widely believed to be rare — and history has proven Franklin's error in this instance. While the Boston physicians were largely and publicly arrayed against the practice, the prevailing religious establishment was for once riding the wave of science and of the future. In any case, James Franklin got around the colonial government's prohibition by simply substituting the name of Benjamin for his own on the masthead of the paper. In the issue of 4 February 1723, it was explained that "The late Publisher of this paper, finding so many Inconveniences would arise by his carrying the Manuscripts and publick News to be supervis'd by the Secretary, as to render his carrying it on unprofitable, has intirely dropt the Undertaking."

Thus, while John Peter Zenger has deservedly become a hero of journalists everywhere, a good case could be made that James Franklin deserves equal, if not higher, billing. He, too, went to jail—a dozen years before Zenger—for publishing an officially distasteful truth. Franklin, however, was released without trial, so that there was no public and legal vindication of his actions. It should also be noted that Franklin's paper was the first effort in America to provide genuine rivalry among news media. Nowhere had there been an effective alternative source of news before; James Franklin was the first American to have the bravery to enter into this dangerous arena.

There being several ways to skin cats, inventive journalists learned long ago that one of the most effective devices to overcome opposition is to incite laughter at the expense of one's opponents. Benjamin Franklin, who did not achieve his exalted place in American history because he lacked talent, imagination or the capacity for hard work, made full use of this tactic. Thus the *New England Courant* also became the first American newspaper to publish essays, letters and commentary.

As noted earlier, the *Courant* continued under the intermittent presence of the elder Franklin until he finally left Massachusetts Bay in 1726 to settle in Newport, then the principal city of the Providence Plantations. Ink was in his blood stream, however, and in 1732 he started the *Rhode Island Gazette*, the first newspaper in that colony. Unfortunately, it lived only for three months, and Franklin, himself, survived it by less than three years.

There was a degree of supportive unanimity among colonial journalists, even though the American Newspaper Publishers Association was a century and a half in the future, for when James Franklin's liberties were under fire in Boston, Andrew Bradford in Pennsylvania editorialized in support of his position in his *American Weekly Mercury* of 19 February 1722: "My Lord Coke[1] observes, That to punish first and then enquire, the Law abhors; but here Mr. Franklin has had a severe Sentence pass'd upon him, even to taking away Part of his Livelihood, without being call'd to make Answer. An indifferent Person would judge by this vote against Couranto, That the Assembly of the Province of Massachusetts Bay are made up of Oppressors and Bigots, who make Religion the only Engine of Destruction to the People…. Thus much we could not forbear saying, out of Compassion to the distressed People of the Province, who must now resign all Pretences to Sense and Reason, and submit to the Tyranny of Priestcraft and Hypocrisy."

As the cause of liberty simmered ever more vigorously among the colonies, and as James Franklin's case made clear, newspapers were hardly popular with colonial authority, unless they could be operated by safe hands. Typical of both the officials and their oppressive attitudes was the reputed statement of Virginia's Governor William Berkeley in 1671: "I thank God we have no free schools or printing; and hope that we shall not have them these hundred years. For learning has brought disobediences and heresy and sects into the world; and printing has divulged them and libels against the government. God keep us from both."[2]

Colonial papers, patterned after those in the mother country, were generally small in size and limited in scope. Harris's *Publick Occurrences*, for example, consisted of only four pages (with the fourth left blank) and was printed on a sheet of paper only six-by-ten inches. Harris stated, in his only issue, that he planned his paper to appear once a month "or if any Glut of Occurrences happen, oftener." As surviving samples of most colonial papers show, the type was well-worn and space was at a premium. Paper and ink were costly — even more so after enactment of the Stamp Act in 1765.[3] But on the whole the colonial newspapers appear to have been reasonably profitable, for many of them stayed in business for decades.

Revenue was from the same two major sources as at present — advertising and subscriptions. Given some differences in the goods and products, their advertisements were not totally dissimilar in type from those carried by present day news media, publicizing everything from patent medicines, bear baitings, slaves (and other property) for sale, and lion exhibitions to the latest London fashions and even summer seminar classes. In its issue of 18 December 1727, the Boston *Gazette* carried a typical advertisement for an obviously much-needed human remedy:

> To be sold, an Excellent Medicine, which cures the Cholick, Dry Belly-ack, Loss of Limbs, Fevers and Agues, Asthmas, Coughs, and all sorts of Obstructions, Rheumatism, Sickness at the Stomach, Surfeits by Immoderate Eating and Drinking, Weakness, Trembling of the Heart, want of Appetite, Gravel, Melancholy, and Jaundice, and is Excellent for the Gout; which is now Published at the desire of several Persons of Note (who have been wonderfully reliev'd by it)....

Subscription income, however, the publisher's other major source of revenue, always seemed a problem. Witness the plaintive and melancholy tone of the notice that John Zenger, son of John Peter, felt obliged to print (on his even more well-worn pica) only a year before he was forced to suspend publication:

> The country subscribers are earnestly entreated to send in their arrears; if they do not pay promptly, I shall leave off sending the paper, and try to recover my money otherwise. Some of these easy subscribers are in arrears for more than seven years. After serving them for so long, I fancy it is time, and high time, that they should repay me my advances; for the truth is — and they may believe me- — I have worn my clothes threadbare.
> N.B. Gentlemen, if you have no money to spare, still think of your printer. When you have read this Advertisement, and thought on it, you cannot do less than say, "Come wife!" (I address myself principally to married folk, but let bachelors take it to heart also), "Come, wife, let us send the poor printer some flour, or a few hams, butter, cheese, poultry, etc."

Nevertheless, as presses proliferated west of the Atlantic, papers began to spring up in the other, less densely populated colonies. Among these, probably the most idealistic was that of Samuel Keimer,[4] publisher of Philadelphia, who published an advance prospectus in October 1728 for his *Universal Instructor in All Arts and Sciences; and Pennsylvania Gazette*. Keimer tried to live up to his masthead by printing extracts from Chambers *Dictionary*, which would have taken him fifty years to complete. But the futility of hoping to meet his payroll with such an ambitious undertaking among a semiliterate populace soon caused him to sell out to the more practical-minded Benjamin Franklin.[5] The new proprietor promptly cut the sheet's name down to manageable size and began his long and laborious climb to everlasting distinction among American printers, patriots and men of learning.

In 1727, William Parks, recently emigrated from England, got himself appointed official government printer for Maryland and promptly established the *Maryland Gazette* in Annapolis.[6] However, after several years of intermittent publication and obviously some financial distress, Parks migrated to the more prosperous environment of Williamsburg and, again designated as the official public printer, in 1736 brought out the *Virginia Gazette*, the first newspaper in that jurisdiction. In South Carolina, the *South Carolina Weekly Journal*, that province's first paper, appeared in 1730, printed by a transplanted New Englander. It was met with the same enthusiasm as was to be shown a number of other Yankee concepts in future years and was superseded two years later by the *South Carolina Gazette*, a journal which lasted for eighty years.

Thus stood the American news media situation at the time John Peter Zenger came onto the field. After Zenger's vindication, the field of journalism seemed a little clearer and more players got into the act. In New England, though James Franklin's Rhode Island paper had died early on, his son tried again in 1758 with the *Newport Mercury*, which fortunately enjoyed a considerably longer life. Similar printed news media soon came into existence in all the other colonies, with the lonesome exception of New Jersey, where local news media have, to this day, remained less effective because of the overbearing but out-of-state presence of the major metropolitan centers of New York and Philadelphia. The *Connecticut Gazette* appeared in New Haven in 1755; the *North Carolina Gazette* in New Bern that same year; the *Wilmington Chronicle* in Delaware in 1762 and the *Georgia Gazette* in Savannah in 1763. Farther north, the *New Hampshire Gazette* appeared in Portsmouth in 1755, but within a decade its editor found himself in trouble for having criticized the actions of both the Continental Congress and the colonial legislature. For this temerity, the editor was publicly censured by a vote of that same legislature, but no further attempt was made to reduce him to obedience.

By the time of the adoption of the United States Constitution in 1789, there were competing printers and newspapers in every major city and journals of some sort in many smaller localities as well. The collective part of these scores of media in securing adoption of the First Amendment cannot be underestimated.

VI
Setting the Stage
Events Leading Up to the Trial of August 1735

The feud between the Van Dam and Morris faction and the governor smoldered vigorously behind all the events that culminated in the arrest and trial of John Peter Zenger. It was a complicated situation, fueled by egos and sparkling with public insults. However, once several members of the faction had been elected to the assembly and were thus in safe positions to speak vigorously, the chorus of criticism against Governor Cosby became more intense. Joining now in the opposition were a number of other prominent citizens, including Gerardus Stuyvesant, grandson of the last Dutch governor; Vincent Mathews, a prosperous upriver landowner; members of the Livingston family, of whom Philip was to become a member of the Continental Congress; and even the prestigious Cadwallader Colden, an otherwise loyal local landowner of considerable consequence.[1] Colden's presence among the disaffected was significant and came about because the security of some of his property holdings in an area recently ceded to New York by Connecticut known as "the Oblong"[2] had also been jeopardized by the convoluted and self-serving machinations of Cosby's minion, Francis Harison. These people and their numerous associates were supported and fueled in their verbal battles by the two highly competent lawyers that had already been engaged by Van Dam, William Smith and James Alexander.

From their new places in the assembly and thus, in accordance with parliamentary precedent, immune from indictment or prosecution by the governor, Lewis Morris and his associates opened vocal inquiries into a number of spicy items — all of which were thoroughly reported in the *New York Weekly Journal*. What were the proprieties involved in Governor Cosby's having accepted a £1,000 honorarium from the assembly merely for opposing renewal of the infamous Sugar Act, the

Cadwallader Colden

extension of which would have worked to the disadvantage of commercial interests in New York?[3] That was only his duty, and to accept this payment was contrary to his instructions. What sort of loyalty had been demonstrated to His Majesty the King when the governor allowed an enemy (French) vessel to reprovision and take on fresh water in New York harbor? Was there a personal payoff for that blatant act of treason? From the security of their legislative positions, the opposition posed these and other embarrassing questions, while the *Journal,* under the skillful wordsmithery of Alexander, blew these juicy tidbits into a series of front-page embarrassments.

Today, two unrelated points still shine clearly through the murk of the intervening years. Each side in these disputes tried to outdo the other in professing loyalty to "the best of all kings." Even if the ruler was felt in the privacy of one's heart to be a knave of the worst sort, such a thought was never said in public — yet. It is clear, in hindsight, that the foes of Governor Cosby had enormous confidence in the persistence and courage of their printer. During Zenger's trial, no evidence was ever produced or even hinted at to the effect that he was merely a puppet typesetter whose journalistic product was the work of others — despite the offering of a relatively enormous reward for anyone who would tattle on him. Thus he became not only a willing participant in the game that unfolded, but indeed its key and star player. In so doing he set the example for all subsequent journalists never to disclose or embarrass your sources.

Every issue of Zenger's *Journal* contained contributions supplied by the Morris faction that were always carefully written so that Zenger was the only legal and obvious publisher. These articles contained essays on liberty of thought, freedom of speech and related topics. They were either reprinted, with credit, from Addison and Steele, Trenchard and Gordon ("Cato") or composed for the occasion by James Alexander, though apparently submitted to the editor over a variety of sham names in the manner of Benjamin Franklin's "Silence Dogood" letters. While these essays formed the heart of the governor's ultimate case against Zenger and may well have struck him as the most vicious, they were only part of the fun that Alexander and his coterie were having at Cosby's expense.

The *Journal* carried real advertisements — it was, after all, in business — but it also carried make-believe ads. Some of these were delightful — if you disliked Cosby and his friends. Understandably, though, the governor found them highly annoying (to say the least). One such was an ad for a lost spaniel that could only be interpreted, by the insiders anyway, as referring to Francis Harison, by now well understood to be one of Cosby's closest cronies as de facto editor of the *New York Gazette*. Another spurious ad depicted the governor himself as a monkey, without, of course, actually mentioning any names. The governor's frustration grew in proportion to the press buildup, and the Van Dam case which started it all disappeared into the distant background.

Stung regularly and repeatedly by the opposition newspaper, Cosby sought to have Zenger indicted by a grand jury in January 1734. The charge was the now commonplace "seditious libel" that had been used in numerous instances for over two centuries to describe the actions of critics of government policy. This time, by way of refinement, the government noted in its accusation that the libels "had recently been circulating in the province"—a backhanded tribute to the popularity of Zenger's paper. The nineteen members of the grand jury, however, refused to find anything wrong with whatever had been circulating and brought no indictment. Governor Cosby was forced back to the political and legal drawing board.

The governor and his attorney general also knew they had another problem, one that lingered as a dangerous precedent. In January 1707, during the years Lord Cornbury was governor, one Francis MacKemie had been charged with "unlicensed preaching" in New York, "with the intent to pervert the church and the government of the province." A clergyman of the disapproved Presbyterian faith, MacKemie had already had a similar run-in with the governmental establishment of Virginia. When brought to trial in New York, MacKemie had admitted to the "preaching" but contended that he had broken no law in the process. The chief justice of the province (Morris' predecessor and thus not a party in Zenger's case), had allowed the jury to return a "general" verdict. This meant that the jury had been allowed to decide both the fact of the case and the law that pertained to it as well. Thus, Cosby was rightfully unsure of the outcome at the hands of an honestly selected jury of Zenger's peers. MacKemie, incidentally, though acquitted by the jury in 1707, had been required to pay court costs of £38.

By the time of the next sitting of a grand jury in October 1734, things had gotten even more tense for His Excellency. The Morrisites had composed a number of victory songs as a result of their electoral triumphs, and these had been printed for public enjoyment. While the "songs" bore no identification of their printer, it was reasonably common knowledge that they had stemmed from Zenger's press. Chief Justice DeLancey brought these new "libels" before the October grand jury with a request they indict the perpetrator. This time the jurors gave the appearance of being in a more cooperative mood. After due deliberation, the foreman announced that the jury was prepared to hand up an indictment, but protested that despite all their collective diligence they could find no evidence as to who was the author, printer or publisher and therefore did not know whom to indict. Soon thereafter a formal proclamation was issued:

> WHEREAS by the Contrivance of some evil Disposed and Disaffected Persons, divers Journals or Printed News-Papers (entitled *The New York Weekly Journal, containing the freshest Advices, foreign and Domestick*) have been caused to be Printed and Published by *John Peter Zenger*, in many of which Journals or Printed News-

Papers (but more particularly in those numbered 7, 47, 48, 49) are contained divers Scandalous, Virulent, False and Seditious Reflections, not only upon the whole Legislature, in general, and upon the most considerable Persons in the most distinguish'd Stations in the Province, but also upon his Majesty's lawful and rightful Government, and just Prerogative. Which said Reflections seem contrived by the Wicked Authors of them, not only to create Jealousies, Discontents and Animosities in the Minds of his Majesty's Liege People of this Province to the Subversion of the Peace and Tranquillity thereof but to alienate their Affection from the best of Kings, and raise *Factions*, *Tumults* and *Sedition* among them. Wherefore I have thought fit, by and with the Advice of his Majesty's Council, to issue this Proclamation, hereby Promising a Reward of *Fifty Pounds*[4] to such Person or Persons who shall discover the Author or Authors of said Scandalous, Virulent and Seditious Reflections contained in the said Journals or Printed News-Papers, to be paid to the said Person or Persons discovering the same as soon as such Author shall have been convicted of having been the Author or Authors thereof.

Given under my Hand and Seal at Fort George,[5] in New York, the sixth day of November, in the 8th year of his Majesty's Reign, Anno Domini, 1734.

W. COSBY

No informants, however, stepped forward to claim the reward.

After this second setback in following normal court procedures, the governor decided to take things out of the hands of the recalcitrant freeholders of New York and to move against Zenger on his own. Governor Cosby caused his attorney general, Richard Bradley, to file "an information" as a way of getting around the refusal of the grand jury to issue an effective indictment. When this "information" was presented to Justices DeLancey and Philipse, they moved with a bench warrant for Zenger's arrest, hoping by this means to cure the ongoing tribulation of a bad but popular press. In this, they were doomed to a further disappointment, but not before they had an adventurous court proceeding on their hands. Meantime, Cosby had lodged a formal complaint with the Board of Trade[6] in London that shows how clearly he saw through Zenger to the forces behind him, even though he realized it was useless to try to prove such a point before a local jury. His complaint stated that James Alexander was abusing him and "maintaining" a press that swarmed "with the most virulent libels." Thus it is manifest that if Zenger had ever given his accusers a hint that he might verify such an accusation, he would have promptly gone home, a free man.

Gouverneur Morris

Immediately following Zenger's arrest in November 1734, Lewis Morris journeyed to England to plead with the secretary of state, the Duke of Newcastle, for a change in royal governors. Interestingly, he got no immediate result from this appeal, though the House of Lords did agree that Cosby's "reasons for removing him [as Chief Justice] were insufficient." Morris also made an impression in London, a result that was no doubt bolstered by the obvious discontent rippling through several of the colonies. When Cosby died in early 1736, he was succeeded

Lewis Morris, first lord of Morrisania

by George Clarke; but two years later, when New Jersey was again set off as a separate colony, Lewis Morris was appointed its governor. Not unexpectedly, Morris lost considerable standing among the circles of discontent by accepting this appointment, but his oldest grandson, Lewis, signed the Declaration of Independence, and his youngest grandson, Gouverneur, was a prime architect of the Constitution of the United States as well as the earliest and most prominent person to appreciate the value and valor of Zenger's case: "The trial of Zenger in 1735 was the germ of American freedom, the morning star of that liberty which subsequently revolutionized America.[7]"

As reports of his difficulties began to reach London, Cosby sought to divert Newcastle by telling him that the difficulties continually boiling up in the province of Massachusetts were "spirited up from home by Mr. Pulteney[8] and that faction," and that he was "sorry to inform your Grace, that ye example and spirit of the Boston people begins to spread among these colonies in a most prodigious manner. I had more trouble to manage these people than I could have imagined." The "home rule" issue was heating up.

As Zenger languished in New York's Old Jail from mid–November through the next grand jury session in January, still under no formal indictment, his friends could see they were heading into a stacked courtroom, where the governor's judges were determined to prevail with every judicial trick they could muster. As we will see in Chapter VII, the first overt sign of that determination was the clerk of the court's attempt to arrange for a very carefully picked jury. Though the clerk was caught almost "red-handed" in the process and had to back off, this event served as a warning to Smith and Alexander that they would need legal reinforcements, and they began to search for help.

The well-known Philadelphia attorney, John Kinsey, was approached for the task of assisting in the defense of Zenger, but since he had been involved with Cosby on other matters he felt there might be a conflict of interest and begged off. As things turned out, they found an even better option, just barely in time. Andrew Hamilton (1676–1741), a native of Scotland, had been attorney general of Pennsylvania from 1717 to 1724 and had become speaker of the colonial assembly in 1729. A distinguished legal scholar and member of the bench of Gray's Inn, he was also an amateur architect who designed "Province House," the building in Philadelphia later known as Independence Hall. Now almost sixty years of age,[9] he was probably the most famous practicing attorney in the colonies, and he was more than willing to help.

Hamilton journeyed to Virginia in 1697 under the assumed name of Trent in order to escape from the dragnet that followed the foiled plot of Sir George Blaylock to kill King William and restore the Stuarts. Befriended by preacher MacKemie, he was soon well-received everywhere for his ability. Hamilton was engaged by the Calverts to formulate the basic legal structure of Maryland, and later he became counsel to the Penn family. His unique position as a "bench" of Gray's Inn also carried a lot of clout. London's four Inns of Court (Lincoln's, Gray's, Inner Temple and Middle Temple) amounted to the bar schools of the British Empire, and those who ran them — the benches — were the equivalent of bar examiners. Without the seal of approval from the

New York's Old Jail, after conversion to the Hall of Records

benches of one of these Inns, no applicant could practice as a barrister before any British court. As the only such person in the colonies, Hamilton was singularly positioned to demand respect from judges, advocates and juries alike.

But, like everyone else in this affair — except Zenger, whose position was little different from that of any press owner — Hamilton had his own personal reasons for participating in the matter. The establishment press in New York was still published by William Bradford; in Philadelphia, the *American Weekly Mercury* was published by his son Andrew and, though also officially sanctioned, had become a thorn in the side of the elected Pennsylvania Assembly — so much so that five years earlier Hamilton had initiated a suit against the younger Bradford for libeling that body. Andrew Bradford had survived Hamilton's suit and then had continued to give the assembly leadership more unfavorable attention than they cared for. A chance to visit New York and perhaps help the competition of the elder Bradford's royalist (i.e., pro-Hanover) press was an opportunity too good to pass up. Andrew Hamilton packed his bag for the trip and brought with him an argument that had been used — unsuccessfully in 1692 in the defense, somewhat ironically, of a much younger William Bradford, then a printer in Philadelphia.

In his defense, Bradford had contended that the members of the jury should be the determinors of both fact and law in cases of this nature. Though this argument had not worked in 1692 before the Philadelphia court, in the intervening forty-four years the preachments of "Cato" and others had altered public opinion to some extent. In the climate of New York in 1735, it was worth another shot. Meantime, and since the *New York Weekly Journal* was still being published thanks to the diligence of Anna Zenger, the staff writers of the Morris and Van Dam faction kept up a steady drumbeat of articles aimed at informing the freeholder jury pool of New York — only about one thousand strong — of their rights and duties under the prevailing laws of libel.

The stage was now set and the significance of the forthcoming drama already well understood by those close to the situation. But it would remain for Governeur Morris, years later, to so eloquently express this significance by calling it "the germ of American freedom."

Judges in the English colonies were traditionally selected by the governors from the upper social, political and economic crust of the pertinent province; most of them had been born in England; many owned extensive properties and fine houses with expensive furniture, fixtures and other luxuries. In contemporary Massachusetts, for example, over half of the colonial judges in the period from 1700 to 1750 sat for their portraits. In this same period, however, their caseloads were increasing dramatically; in Massachusetts, caseload relative to population increased from 1.31 per thousand in 1710 to 5.78 per thousand in 1730, a period in which population also grew by some 40 percent.

Increasingly as the eighteenth century progressed, judges were put in the position of defending the actions of inept and unpopular royal officials, policies and institutions. As talk of rebellion increased after the Sugar Act of 1764 and the Stamp Act of the following year,[10] court procedures became even more chaotic, and in the most turbulent of the colonies, Massachusetts, there was even a colony-wide jurors' strike in 1774. Of course, the provision in both the Sugar Act and the Stamp Act for infractions to be tried in Admiralty Courts, rather than before a jury of one's peers, was a primary cause of great disaffection.

Court days in colonial America were also festive occasions. In some rural areas, when the practicing justices were expected to arrive for their periodic assizes, they were met at the edge of town with bands and banners to be formally escorted to the town hall or to the most impressive meeting place in the area. There, court would be convened with the traveling judges arrayed in all their judicial finery. At certain times of year, particularly during the slower winter months when farmers had time on their hands, court proceedings were often the equivalent of today's going out to the movies. Trials were commonly regarded as the best entertainment of the year, particularly if the participating barristers were known to have the talent necessary to put on a good show.

Arrayed in their scarlet robes of finest English broadcloth, with white cambric trim and ornate fringes, crowned overall with their immense white wigs, judges were quite a sight. Those who argued before them were only somewhat less flamboyant. Barristers wore the required but more subdued costume of their trade — black gowns, cambric banding and generally the less impressive tie wigs. All of these elegant costumes were part of the aura designed to give the judicial process an air of solemnity, dignity and pomp, to inspire the populace with sufficient awe and majesty that any resulting decisions would be layered with enough respect to command the public support necessary to keep outspoken parties in a compliant frame of mind. Zenger's trial demonstrated all of these elements — and a "pro bono" lawyer of continental standing.

Coincidentally, Bradford, the "official" printer to the province, was at this time having his own troubles, though they never reached the courtroom. In 1735 one Joseph Johnson was apprehended and charged with the counterfeit printing of ten shilling provincial bills. Counterfeiting was getting to be big business, largely headquartered in various swamps among the woods of the Oblong. To escape prosecution and the possibility of having his ears cropped or worse, Johnson fled to New Jersey, abandoning his wife and six-year-old child. Tried in absentia, it turned out that he (like Zenger) had learned his trade from Bradford. Notwithstanding, he was adjudged guilty, and his son, rather than become a public burden, was also apprenticed to Bradford.

VII
Trial Preliminaries

Like many another hero, John Peter Zenger obviously did not originally intend to embark on a course as risky and uncomfortable as his became. But once into the game, this hero, like the folk hero Arnold von Winkelried at the 1386 Battle of Sempach Lake, insisted on playing through to the end.[1] Zenger stood firmly by his original commitment, and despite nine months spent in prison awaiting trial he never faltered in staying the course. As events turned out, he thus became more than a much-needed but merely mechanical pawn in the power struggle for the minds of New Yorkers that raged between the Governor's faction and the "Morrisites" (a group which by now included almost every influential person disaffected by Cosby's avarice and high-handedness). But, with time, the far-reaching significance of Zenger's courage became a prominent landmark in the evolution of human freedom.

Other than some understandable editorial rejoicing at his arrest, Zenger's trial was hardly covered by the opposition medium, but due to the literary skill and advocacy of his backers — and to the competent devotion of Anna Catherine, his wife, the *Journal* continued its publication, missing only one issue during the long months that Zenger languished in the jail cell. Zenger himself explained the situation in the issue of 25 November 1734[2]:

> As you last week were Disappointed of my Journall, I think it incumbent upon me, to publish my Apology which is this. On the Lord's Day, the Seventh of this Instant, I was Arrested, taken and Imprisoned in the common Gaol of this City, by Virtue of a Warrant from the *Governor*, and the Honourable *Francis Harrison*, Esq; and others in Council of which (God willing) you'l have a Copy, whereupon I was put under such Restraint that I had not the Liberty of Pen, Ink, or Paper, or to see, or speak with People, till upon my Complaint to the Honourable the Chief Justice, at my appearing before him upon my *Habeas Corpus* on the *Wednesday* following.

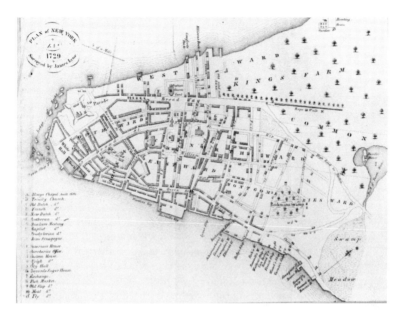

Plan of New York City in 1729

Who discountenanced that Proceeding, and therefore I have had since that Time, the Liberty of Speaking through the Hole of the Door, to my Wife and Servants by which I doubt not you'l think me sufficiently Excused for not sending my last week's *Journal* and I hope for the future by the Liberty of Speaking to my Servants thro' the Hole of the Door of the Prison, to entertain you with my weekly *Journall* as formerly.

Zenger's imprisonment had unforeseen beneficial side effects. His circulation jumped dramatically, straining the capacity of his staff, which must have been a pleasant enough problem. In addition, Bradford's *Gazette* was compelled to print articles and notices on Zenger, a practice regarded with horror by most publishers, who seldom care to set the names of competitors before the public. However, as the weeks dragged on, some of the articles in the *Gazette* must have stung, and his morale must have suffered — witness parts of a composition that appeared in his Christmas issue:

From my Prison, December 20th, 1734.

Oh cruelty unknown before
To any barbarous savage shore

> Much more when Men so much profess
> Humanity and Godliness

... That I was brought over at the charitable Expence of the Crown is the only Truth that groaping Fumbler found when he studied that clumsy Performance. I acknowledge it: Thanks be to QUEEN ANNE whose Name I Mention with Reverence, her Bounty to me and my distress'd County [sic] Folks is to be gratefully remembered. If that Author has contributed any Thing towards it, I begg to be informed. I assure him that my Acknowledgement shall not be wanting, notwithstanding his ill Treatment: If he has not, I begg leave to tell him, that it is mean for him to twit me with Benefits that I am in no ways beholden to him for.

That my Friends are pretendedly so, will (I hope)) prove to be as false as my Enemies are malicious; whatever some of my Adversaries may be, I believe my Friends to be Men of Honour and Probity. And if they even should forsake me, I would say of them as *Cicero* said in Answer to the Notions the *Epicureans* had of a God, *si tales sint Amici, ut nulla gratia, nulla hominum, charitate teneantur valeant.*[3] I'll trust to the Laws of the Realm and my country, and still retain my Integrity: FOR HONEST IS THE BEST POLICY....

The courtroom where Zenger's trial took place was on the main floor of the New York City Hall. Three stories high and built in 1699 on the northeast corner of Nassau and Wall Streets, this was still regarded as the finest building in the city; it also served as the meeting place for the semiannual sessions of the provincial assembly. Hintermeister's realistic painting shows the large, high-ceilinged chamber with sun streaming through its tall windows onto a crowded gallery and spectator area. In the foreground, a dozen rapt jurors are gathered around the bewigged figure of Andrew Hamilton as he delivers his closing argument. On the left side, in an enclosed box for all to see, is the accused, dressed for the occasion in his best suit; having spent most of a year away from his press, one can be sure his fingernails were clean. On the other side, elevated several steps above all others, are the two judges behind their ornate bench.[4]

In the height of summer, one can only imagine that the physical heat of the scene was fully as great as the political. Though the earliest sustained and reliable meteorological records of North America were not commenced until 1738 (in Philadelphia), one must still assume that the humidity and temperature within the courtroom would have been sufficient to cause all the bystanders to quickly escape to a cooler clime — had it not been for the popularity of the defendant's cause. In

Old City Hall

any case, the fireplace, traditionally located behind the judge's chairs in colonial court chambers, was definitely not needed on that August day.

Later known as Federal Hall, the old New York City Hall became one of the most historic buildings of the United States. As the meeting place of the first Congress after adoption of the Constitution, the room in which Zenger was tried and acquitted would be a singularly fitting venue for Congressional initiation of the American Bill of Rights. George Washington took his oath of office in this chamber, and, before Congress began to use it, it was substantially remodeled under the supervision of Pierre Charles L'Enfant, the same friend of Lafayette who is credited with later laying out the national capital. Sadly for such a landmark of liberty, the building was torn down in 1812 and the site later occupied by a subtreasury building adjacent to the nation's financial center.

Zenger summed up the background of his trial succinctly enough, describing the unsuccessful attempt in October 1734 to indict him:

> As there was but one printer in the Province of New York who printed a public newspaper, I was in hopes that if I undertook to publish another I might make it worth my while. I soon found my hopes were not groundless. My first paper was printed on November 5, 1733; and I continued printing and publishing them, I thought to the satisfaction of everybody, till the January following,

Andrew Hamilton delivering his closing speech to the jury at the trial of John Peter Zenger

when the Chief Justice was pleased to animadvert upon the doctrine of libels in a long "charge" given in that term to the grand jury. Afterwards, on the third Tuesday of October, 1734, he [DeLancey] was again pleased to charge the grand jury in the following words:

"Gentlemen, I shall conclude with reading a paragraph or two out of the same book concerning libels. They are arrived to that height that they call loudly for your animadversion. It is high time to put a stop to them. For at the rate things are now carried on, when all order and government is endeavored to be trampled on, and reflections are cast upon persons of all degrees, must not these things end in sedition, if not timely prevented? Lenity you have seen will not avail. It becomes you then to inquire after the offenders, that we may in a due course of law be enabled to punish them. If you, gentlemen, do not interpose, consider whether the ill consequences that may arise from any disturbances of the public peace may not in part lie at your door?"

DeLancey continued his charge to the grand jury by quoting from the then leading authority on English law, William Hawkins (1673–1746), a "serjeant at law," who was the author of the *Treatise on the Pleas of the Crown*, first published in 1717, but with many subsequent editions.[5] In the chapter on libels, Judge DeLancey noted, Hawkins considers, first, what shall be said to be a libel and, second, who are liable to be punished for it:

> "Under the first he says: 'Nor can there be any doubt but that a writing which defames a private person only is as much a libel as that which defames persons intrusted in a public capacity, inasmuch as it manifestly tends to create ill blood, and to cause a disturbance of the public peace. However, it is certain that it is a very high aggravation of a libel that it tends to scandalize the government, by reflecting on those who are intrusted with the administration of public affairs; which does not only endanger the public peace, as all other libels do, by stirring up the parties immediately concerned in it to acts of revenge, but also has a direct tendency to breed in the people a dislike of their governors, and incline them to faction and sedition.'"

Continuing to quote from Hawkins, DeLancey went on to his second point, noting those who are liable to be punished for the publication of whatever may be found to be a libel:

> "'It is certain that not only he who composes or procures another to compose it but also that he who publishes, or procures another to publish it, are in danger of being punished for it. And it is not material whether he who dispersed a libel knew anything of the contents or effects of it or not; for nothing could be more easy than to publish the most virulent papers with the greatest security if concealing the purport of them from an illiterate publisher would make him safe in dispersing them.
>
> "These, gentlemen, are some of the offenses which are to make part of your inquiries. If any other should arise in the course of your proceedings, in which you are at a loss or conceive any doubts, upon your application here we will assist and direct you."

As already mentioned, the grand jury failed to indict Zenger — an outcome that was apparently foregone. The governor then asked the members of the Governor's Council (of which DeLancey was one) to ponder on what to do about Zenger's newspaper. Since they could not get an indictment, perhaps there was some way in which the *New York*

Weekly Journal could be legislated out of existence. The Council, therefore, under Cosby's severe prodding, sent a message to the provincial
assembly asking that elective body to appoint a committee to act with
one from the Council.

In due course, the two committees met, but the assembly insisted
that the wishes of the Governor's Council be put into precise language.
This was a wise precaution on the part of the Morrisites, for it required
the governor and his adherents to state their complaint in a form that
would not permit subsequent waffling and alteration. The assembly
very soon received a written response:

> "Gentlemen, the matters we request your concurrence in are that
> Zenger's papers, Nos. 7, 47, 48, 49 — which were read, and which we
> now deliver — be burned by the hands of the common hangman, as
> containing in them many things derogatory of the dignity of His
> Majesty's government, reflecting upon the legislature and upon the
> most considerable persons in the most distinguished stations in the
> Province, and tending to raise seditions and tumults among the
> people thereof.
>
> "That you concur with us in addressing the Governor to issue his
> proclamation with a promise of reward for the discovery of the
> authors or writers of these seditious libels.
>
> "That you concur with us in an order for prosecuting the printer
> thereof.
>
> "That you concur with us in an order to the magistrates to exert
> themselves in the execution of their offices in order to preserve the
> public peace of the Province."

Under the leadership of the Morris and Van Dam faction, and with
very little delay, the assembly flatly refused to agree to any such procedure, and the letter from the Council was returned to it along with the
copies of the *Journal* that had been marked for public burning. Three
weeks later, on Thursday, 22 October 1734, when the newly elected
aldermen and magistrates of the city met the Court of Quarter Sessions
(the quarterly judicial session), Sheriff John Symes delivered as to the
assembled freeholder representatives an order from the governor which
read as follows:

> "Whereas by an order of this Council some of John Peter Zenger's
> journals, entitled *The New York Weekly Journal*, Nos. 7, 47, 48, 49,
> were ordered to be burned by the hands of the common hangman
> or whipper near the pillory in this city on Wednesday the 6th
> between the hours of 11 and 12 in the forenoon, as containing in

them many things tending to sedition and faction, to bring His
Majesty's government into contempt, and to disturb the peace
thereof, and containing in them likewise not only reflections upon
His Excellency the Governor in particular, and the legislature in
general, but also upon the most considerable persons in the most
distinguished stations in this Province;

"It is therefore ordered that the mayor and magistrates (aldermen
sitting in their judicial capacities as Justices of the Peace) of this city
do attend at the burning of the several papers or journals aforesaid,
numbered as above mentioned."

Upon hearing this command, the city magistrates forbade the
entering of it onto their books at that time, and several of those present declared that if it should be entered they would like to have their
personal protests entered as well. Thus rebuffed, the sheriff—a Cosby
appointee—returned the very next day with an order for the Court of
Quarter Sessions to comply. At this point one of the veniremen handed
up a written protest, which was read aloud by the clerk, approved vocif-
erously by many of those present and entered on the court records without protest as follows:

"Whereas an order has been served on this Court;
"And whereas this Court conceives that they are only to be com-
manded by the king's mandatory writs, authorized by law, to which
they conceive that they have the right of showing cause why they
do not obey them if they believe them improper to be obeyed; or
by orders which have some known laws to authorize them;
"And whereas this Court conceives this order to be no mandatory writ warranted by law, nor knows of no law that authorizes
making the order aforesaid, so they think themselves under no
obligation to obey it. Which obedience they think would be in them
the opening of a door for arbitrary commands, which, when once
opened, they know not what dangerous consequences may attend
it;
"Therefore this Court conceives itself bound in duty (for the
preservation of the rights of this Corporation, and, as much as they
can, of the liberty of the press and of the people of the Province,
since the Assembly of the Province and several grand juries have
refused to meddle with the papers when applied to by the Council)
to protest against the order aforesaid, and to forbid all the members of this Corporation to pay any obedience to it until it be shown
to this Court that the same is authorized by some known law, which
they neither know nor believe that it is."

Upon the reading of this truculent rebuff, the court then demanded that Francis Harison, secretary of the colony and member of the Council, who was in the courtroom and had been present at the drawing up of the order, cite the authority under which that order was made. Harison was hardly popular with the freeholders, his greed and connivance relative to the "Oblong" having become a matter of common knowledge and one of the major handicaps to Cosby's political effectiveness. Nevertheless, he spoke up manfully, citing the 1709 case of a sermon preached by Henry Sacheverell (1674–1724), a Tory clergyman (but not a member of Parliament), who had attacked the Whig ministry for not being sufficiently royalist. He was convicted, and the House of Lords ordered the text of his sermon be burned by the hangman and that the mayor and aldermen of London should witness the event. While this alone may have made his point, Harison could have also noted the political sequel — which found the Whig government so embarrassed by the relatively light sentence given Dr. Sacheverell that it soon ran out of parliamentary confidence.

One of the aldermen present clearly knew the whole story and answered Harison fully. He stated that the Zenger and Sacheverell matters were in no way similar because Dr. Sacheverell and his sermon were impeached by the House of Commons of England, the grand jury of the nation and representative of the whole people of England. Their impeachment was prosecuted before the House of Lords, the greatest court of justice of Britain, which has traditionally had jurisdiction of such trials. He also noted that Sacheverell had had a fair hearing in his defense and that Zenger had been given none. After that fair hearing, Sacheverell and his sermon were justly, fairly, and legally condemned.

This alderman, whose name unfortunately was not recorded, had read the details of the Sacheverell case and recalled that in the judgment of the House of Lords only the mayor and sheriffs of London and Middlesex should attend the burning of the sermon, not the aldermen. Finally, he asked that Harison show proof that the governor and his Council had such final authority as the House of Lords and that the papers ordered to be burned were as legally prosecuted and condemned as in the case of Dr. Sacheverell. Without such showings, the alderman's opinion was that a censure ought not to be pronounced, not without a fair trial by a competent and legal authority.

Harison was also asked to produce the citations for his authorities, so that the magistrates might analyze them. He was told that if he could demonstrate sufficient validity to warrant this order they would readily obey it, but not otherwise. His weak response was to the effect that he did not carry his books around with him. Upon which someone suggested that he might send for them or order a constable to fetch them.

Feeling himself defeated, Harison rose to leave, but turned before reaching the door and mentioned that the pastoral letter of Bishop Gilbert Burnett of Salisbury (1643–1715), a member of the House of Commons, had been ordered by the House of Lords to be burned by the high bailiff of Westminster. Whatever relevance this had was unestablished; the letter in question had been one in which the bishop had urged tolerance to those who disagreed with the established church.[6] Harison then marched out without either waiting for an answer or promising to bring his books.

After Harison's departure it was moved that the alderman's protest be entered into their formal transcript. But others observed that the protest could not be entered without entering also the order, and that it was probably best to take no notice of it. Therefore this was followed by a unanimous vote that "[t]he said papers and request do lie upon the table." The sheriff then asked that the court direct the whipper to perform the order to burn Zenger's *Journals*. But another of the aldermen noted that the whipper was an official of the province and that, thus, the aldermen could give no such order. Soon after that the session was adjourned.

The minutes of New York's Common Council are silent on this entire matter — in keeping with its vote. However, the entire group (and all their elected assistants) were present. They deserve a place in the annals of astute political gamesmanship — Mayor Robert Lurting (who had been mayor since 1726, but would not live to see Zenger vindicated), Deputy Mayor Gerardus Stuyvesant (representing the Out Ward), Christopher Fell (Montgomerie Ward), Stephen Bayard (Dock Ward), Simon Johnson (South Ward), William Roome (West Ward), Johannes Burger (North Ward) and John Walter (East Ward).

About noon that day, Sheriff Symes, after reading the numbers of the several papers which were ordered to be burned, directed his own Negro slave to put them in the fire, which he did in the presence of Harison and several of the officers of the garrison from Fort George.

Less than two weeks later, on Sunday, 17 November 1734, Zenger was arrested and imprisoned by virtue of a bench warrant which read as follows:

"At a Council held at Fort George in New York, November 2, 1734. Present: His Excellency William Cosby, Captain General and Governor in Chief, Mr. Clarke, Mr. Harison, Mr. Livingston, Mr.

Kennedy, the Chief Justice [DeLancey], Mr. Cortlandt, Mr. Lane, Mr. Horsmanden.

"It is ordered that the sheriff for the City of New York do forthwith take and apprehend John Peter Zenger for printing and publishing several seditious libels dispersed throughout his journals or newspapers, entitled *The New York Weekly Journal*; as having in them many things tending to raise factions and tumults among the people of this Province, inflaming their minds with contempt of His Majesty's government, and greatly disturbing the peace thereof. And upon his taking the said John Peter Zenger, to commit him to the prison or common jail of the said city and county."

And being by virtue of that warrant so imprisoned in the jail, I was for several days denied the use of pen, ink and paper, and the liberty of speech with any persons.

Some members of the Council were notable for their absence from this politically critical session. Understandably, these included James Alexander, Zenger's lawyer; but significant by his absence was the scholarly Cadwallader Colden and the elderly upcountry landowner, Abraham Van Horne. The accusers were all men of substance at the time and all close supporters of Governor Cosby. George Clarke (1670–1759), secretary to the province after 1703, remained prominent in provincial affairs, succeeding Cosby as governor for seven years after 1736. He had surveyed the boundary line between New York and Connecticut and as a result had done quite well for himself in land speculations along the way. However, he underwent the final indignity of being captured by the French on his way home to England in 1745. Harison has already been introduced, but it is informative to note that when he fled the province in 1735, he was replaced as councillor by George Clarke, Jr. A member of the landed aristocracy, Philip Livingston had been on the Council since 1725 and stayed on it thereafter until his death in 1750. His son and namesake did a little better for the cause of liberty: he sat in the Continental Congress, signed the Declaration of Independence and was among the framers of the U.S. Constitution. Archibald Kennedy (1695–1763) had arrived in New York from his native Scotland in 1710. A sometime pamphleteer, he served as collector of customs after 1722 and bought Bedloe's Island in 1746. He was a member of the Governor's Council from 1727 to 1761. DeLancey had been on the Council since 1729 and stayed on it until his death in 1760, serving for two of those years (1753–1754) as acting governor. He was succeeded by his son, Oliver, who stayed on the Council until 1776, when many things came unglued locally. Philip Cortland, with extensive land holdings north of Morrisania, had replaced Lewis Morris as councillor in 1730 and stayed on the Council until his death in 1746. Henry Lane was the junior councillor, having been appointed by Cosby on his arrival in 1733; he served until his death in 1744. Daniel Horsemanden (1694–1778) was born in England and admitted to the New York bar in 1732. A vestryman of Trinity parish from 1734 to 1772, he was Harison's successor as recorder and also served two terms on the New York Supreme Court —1736–1747 and 1753–1763. He stayed on the Council until the American Revolution (with a hiatus of eight years after 1747, because he fell out of favor with Governor George Clinton).

Zenger's bail was set at a total of £800, such an enormous figure as to be well beyond the means of Zenger himself, but by no means beyond that of his backers. They, however, had determined it better to make a martyr of the printer. This case of exorbitant bail was contrary to the English Bill of Rights of 1689, and, festering thereafter in the minds of many colonists, it was high among the stimulants of the grievances set forth under date of 4 July 1776. The issue was to make a further appearance in the Eighth Amendment to the Constitution. Van Dam's lawyers, James Alexander and William Smith, now appearing for Zenger, made a plea of habeas corpus and then argued before the court that their client had a right to reasonable bail. In support of their case, they appealed to English law and precedent.

Zenger offered an affidavit on his net worth — not counting the tools of his trade and wearing apparel, he could weigh in at only £40. Despite the authorities cited and the arguments produced by his counsel proving Zenger's right to moderate bail, such as was within his power to give, Chief Justice DeLancey and his colleague Philipse were adamant. Zenger described the situation modestly:

> Some warm expressions (to say no worse of them) were dropped on this occasion, sufficiently known and resented by the listeners, which for my part I desire may be buried in oblivion. In the end it was ordered that I might be admitted to bail, myself in 400 pounds with two sureties, each in 200 pounds, and that I should be remanded till I gave it.
>
> As this was ten times more than was in my power to countersecure any person in giving bail for me, I conceived that I could not ask any to become my bail on these terms; and therefore I returned to the jail, where I lay until Tuesday, January 28, 1735, the last day of the court term. Then, the grand jury having found nothing against me, I expected to be discharged from my imprisonment. But

my hopes proved vain, for the attorney general then charged me by "information" for printing and publishing parts of my *Journals* Nos. 13 and 23 as being "false, scandalous, malicious and seditious."

When the Court reconvened on 15 April 1735, Alexander and Smith rose to dispute the propriety of DeLancey and Philipse presiding over the trial of this case. Counsel took the position that the commissions of DeLancey and Philipse were defective because, among other things, Governor Cosby had himself appointed the two judges, without the consent of his council, and they thus served "at pleasure" instead of "during good behavior." By way of further exception, these judges' impartiality was clearly suspect because they had been parties to the bringing of the suit against Zenger in the first place. The *Journal* reported that:

> Alexander offered the above "exceptions" to the Court and asked that they might be heard in argument. Upon this the Chief Justice warned them that they ought well to consider the consequences of what they offered. Both lawyers answered that they had done so, as well as all the consequences. Smith added that he was so well satisfied of his right to take an exception to the commission of a judge, if he thought such commission illegal, that he would venture his life on the point. As to the validity of the exceptions offered, he was ready to argue them, too, if the court was willing to hear him. DeLancey replied that he would consider the exceptions in the morning, and ordered the clerk to bring them to him.

However, the court offered no hearing or other opportunity for Alexander and Smith to make their case about the questionable impartiality or competence of the judges:

> On Wednesday, April 16, the Chief Justice delivered one of the exceptions to the clerk, and to Justice Philipse the other, upon which Mr. Smith arose and asked the judges whether the court would hear him. DeLancey responded from the bench that the court would neither hear nor allow the exceptions. "For," said he, "you thought to have gained a great deal of applause and popularity by opposing this Court; but you have brought it to that point that either we must go from the bench or you from the bar. Therefore we exclude you and Mr. Alexander from the bar." He delivered a paper to the clerk and ordered it to be entered, which the clerk entered accordingly, and

returned the paper to the Chief Justice. After which the Chief Justice ordered the clerk to read publicly what he had written.

Alexander and Smith were reinstated in their practice of law in 1737 — but only by act of the provincial legislature not as a result of calmer afterthought by the usually affable DeLancey.

VIII
Jury Selection and Opening Arguments

> James Alexander and William Smith, attorneys of this Court, having presumed, notwithstanding they were forewarned by the Court of their displeasure if they should do it, to sign, and having actually signed and put into Court, exceptions in the name of John Peter Zenger, thereby denying the legality of the judges' commissions (though in the usual form) and the being of this Supreme Court;
>
> It is therefore ordered that, for the said contempt, the said James Alexander and William Smith be excluded from any farther practice in this Court, and that their names be struck out of the roll of attorneys of this Court.

After the order was read, on that sixteenth of April, Alexander asked whether it was the order of Justice Philipse as well as of the Chief Justice. Both judges answered that it was indeed their order. Alexander added that it was proper to ask by what means they might make an appeal; he further observed that the court had made a mistake in its wording because the exceptions were only to DeLancey's and Philipse's commissions, not to the very existence of the court, and asked that the order might be altered accordingly. DeLancey replied that the justices had conceived that the exceptions were against the being of the court. Both Alexander and Smith denied that they were and prayed the Chief Justice to point to the place that contained such exception. They noted that the court might well exist even though the commissions of all the judges were void; a situation which the Chief Justice confessed to be true. Therefore the two attorneys prayed again that the order in that point might be altered — but to no avail.

Two days later Alexander and Smith asked the court for a ruling on the extent to which they were affected by the court order. They mentioned that there was some question whether, by the words of the order, they were debarred from their practice both as counsel as well as attorneys; they "practiced" in both capacities. DeLancey answered, with Philipse concurring, that the order was plain: James Alexander and William Smith were debarred and excluded from their whole practice at this bar; the order was intended to bar their acting both as counsel and as attorneys, and it could not be construed otherwise.

Without doubt this punishment succeeded in terrorizing the balance of the established lawyers in New York. However, upon this exclusion of his counsel, Zenger asked the court to order new counsel for his defense. Thereupon the court appointed John Chambers (1710–1765), a newly fledged lawyer who had been an assistant alderman in 1731 and one of the signers of a recent encomium complimenting the administration of Governor Cosby. In due course, Chambers would become a prominent lawyer in New York, a justice of the Supreme Court, a delegate to the colonial congress that met in Albany in 1754 and even a member of the Council for a dozen years after 1753. But at this time, he was utterly without courtroom experience. Nevertheless, he did the honorable thing and pleaded "not guilty" for his client. As to whether the exceptions entered by Alexander and Smith should be part of the record, Chambers thought it better not to speak about the matter.

Chambers asked that a definite trial date be established and moved for a struck jury. In this traditional procedure, the sheriff furnished a list of forty-eight names taken randomly from the total list of freeholders. Of the total, each side was entitled to strike up to twelve names, leaving half. From the remaining twenty-four, a twelve man jury was selected by the traditional voir dire. Trial was ordered to begin on Monday, 4 August, but the court would consider till the first day of that midsummer term whether Zenger would be allowed a struck jury or not.

Although Zenger went back to his cell, his *A Brief Narrative of the Case and Trial of John Peter Zenger* (1736) carried the story in specific detail from that point. Publication of this full account of his trial was delayed for ten months after his acquittal because the various lawyers took a long time to go over their notes and correct his manuscript; but when it finally appeared, the resulting document was a book-sized edition that was immediately reprinted in Boston and Philadelphia, was excerpted in several other colonial publications and went through five editions in London.[1] The next stage of the trial, jury selection, which began with the start of the midsummer term, commences in Zenger's *Narrative* thus:

On Tuesday, July 29, 1735, the Court opened. On the motion of Mr. Chambers for a struck jury, pursuant to the rule of the preceding term, the Court were of the opinion that I was entitled to have a struck jury. That evening at five o'clock some of my friends attended the clerk for striking the jury; when to their surprise the clerk [Harison], instead of producing the Freeholders book, to strike the jury from it in their presence as usual, produced a list of 48 persons whom he said he had taken out of the Freeholders book.

My friends told him that a great number of these persons were not freeholders; that others were persons holding commissions and offices at the Governor's pleasure; that others were of the late displaced magistrates of this city, who must be supposed to have resentment against me for what I had printed concerning them; that others were the Governor's baker, tailor, shoemaker, candlemaker, joiner, etc.; that as to the few indifferent men that were upon that list, they had reason to believe (as they had heard) that Mr. Attorney had a list of them, to strike them out. And therefore they requested that he would either bring the Freeholders book, and choose out of it 48 unexceptional men in their presence as usual, or else that he would hear their objections particularly to the list he offered, and that he would put impartial men in the place of those against whom they could show just objections.

Notwithstanding this, the clerk refused to strike the jury out of the Freeholders book, and refused to hear any objections to the persons on the list; but told my friends that if they had any objections to any persons, they might strike those persons out. To which they answered that there would not remain a jury if they struck out all the exceptional men, and according to the custom they had a right to strike out only twelve.

Finding no arguments could prevail with the clerk to hear their objections to his list, nor to strike the jury as usual, Mr. Chambers told him that he must apply to the Court; which the next morning he did. And the Court upon his motion ordered that the 48 should be struck out of the Freeholders book as usual, in the presence of the parties, and that the clerk should hear objections to persons proposed to be of the 48, and allow of such exceptions as were just. In pursuance of that order a jury was that evening struck to the satisfaction of both parties. My friends and counsel insisted on no objections but want of freehold, although they did not insist that Mr. Attorney General should show any particular cause against any persons he disliked, but acquiesced that any person he disliked should be left out of the 48.

A satisfactory jury having finally been selected, Zenger's account of the actual court proceedings immediately begins to show the extent of the official bias against him. For a second time, Harison, as clerk, attempted to rig the jury; but, inexperienced as he was, Chambers honorably and effectively protected his client, and subsequently the trial began in earnest:

> Before James DeLancey, Chief Justice of the Province of New York, and Frederick Philipse, Associate Justice, my trial began on August 4, 1735, upon an information for printing and publishing two newspapers which were called libels against our Governor and his administration.
>
> The defendant, John Peter Zenger, being called, appeared.
>
> MR. CHAMBERS, of counsel for the defense. "I humbly move, Your Honors, that we may have justice done by the sheriff, and that he may return the names of the jurors in the same order as they were struck."
>
> MR. CHIEF JUSTICE. "How is that? Are they not so returned?"
>
> MR. CHAMBERS. "No they are not. For some of the names that were last set down in the panel are now placed first."
>
> MR. CHIEF JUSTICE. "Make that out and you shall be righted."
>
> MR. CHAMBERS. "I have the copy of the panel in my hand as the jurors were struck, and if the clerk will produce the original signed by Mr. Attorney and myself, Your Honor will see that our complaint is just."
>
> MR. CHIEF JUSTICE. "Clerk, is it so? Look upon that copy. Is it a true copy of the panel as it was struck?"
>
> CLERK. "Yes, I believe it is."
>
> MR. CHIEF JUSTICE. "How came the names of the jurors to be misplaced in the panel?"
>
> SHERIFF. "I have returned the jurors in the same order in which the clerk gave them to me."
>
> MR. CHIEF JUSTICE. "Let the names of the jurors be ranged in the order they were struck, agreeable to the copy here in Court."
>
> Which was done accordingly; and the jury, whose names were as follows, were called and sworn: Thomas Hunt (Foreman), Harmanus Rutgers, Stanly Holmes, Edward Man, John Bell, Samuel Weaver, Andries Marschalk, Egbert van Borsom, Benjamin Hildreth, Abraham Keteltas, John Goelet, Hercules Wendover.[2]
>
> Mr. Attorney General[3] opened the information, which was as follows:
>
> MR. ATTORNEY. "May it please Your Honors and you, Gentlemen of the Jury. The information now before the Court, and to

which the defendant, Zenger, has pleaded 'Not guilty,' is an information for printing and publishing a false, scandalous, and seditious libel in which His Excellency, the Governor of this Province, who is the king's immediate representative here, is greatly and unjustly scandalized as a person that has no regard to law or justice; with much more, as will appear upon reading the information. Libeling has always been discouraged as a thing that tends to create differences among men, ill blood among the people, and oftentimes great bloodshed between the party libeling and the party libeled. There can be no doubt but you, Gentlemen of the Jury, will have the same ill opinion of such practices as judges have always shown upon such occasions. But I shall say no more at this time, until you hear the information, which is as follows:

"Be it remembered that Richard Bradley, Attorney General of the king for the Province of New York, who prosecutes for the king in this part, in his own proper person comes here into the Court of the king, and for the king gives the Court here to understand and be informed:

"That John Peter Zenger, of the City of New York, printer, being a seditious person; and a frequent printer and publisher of false news and seditious libels, both wickedly and maliciously devising the administration of His Excellency William Cosby, Captain General and Governor in Chief, to traduce, scandalize, and vilify both His Excellency the Governor and the ministers and officers of the king, and to bring them into suspicion and the ill opinion of the subjects of the king residing within the Province, on the twenty-eighth day of January, in the seventh year of the reign of George the Second, at the City of New York did falsely, seditiously, and scandalously print and publish, and cause to be printed and published, a certain false, malicious, seditious, scandalous libel entitled *The New York Weekly Journal.*"

Bradley was reading from the prepared "information," but he wanted to make sure that the jury understood the implications of wording used by the *Journal* and thus ad-libbed those parts into his prepared script. They are here recorded by Zenger in parenthesis:

"In which libel, among other things therein contained, are these words, 'Your appearance in print at last gives a pleasure to many, although most wish you had come fairly into the open field, and not appeared behind entrenchments made of the supposed laws against libeling, and of what other men had said and done before. These entrenchments, gentlemen, may soon be shown to you and to all men to be weak, and to have neither law nor reason for their foundation, and so cannot long stand in your stead. Therefore you had much better as yet leave them, and come to what the people of this City and Province (the City and Province of New York meaning) think are the points in question. They (the people of the City and Province of New York meaning) think, as matters now stand, that their liberties and properties are precarious, and that slavery is like to be entailed on them and their posterity if some past things be not amended, and this they collect from many past proceedings." (Meaning many of the past proceedings of His Excellency, the Governor, and of the ministers and officers of the king, of and for the said Province.)

"And the Attorney General likewise gives the Court here to understand and be informed:

"That the said John Peter Zenger afterwards, to wit on the eighth day of April, did falsely, seditiously and scandalously Print and publish another false, malicious, seditious, and Scandalous libel entitled *The New-York Weekly Journal.*

"In which libel, among other things therein contained, are these words, 'one of our neighbors (one of the inhabitants of New Jersey meaning) being in company and observing the strangers (some of the inhabitants of New York meaning) full of complaints, endeavored to persuade them to remove into Jersey.' To which it was replied, 'that would be leaping out of the frying pan into the fire; for,' says he, 'we both are under the same Governor (His Excellency the said Governor meaning), and your Assembly have shown with a vengeance what is to be expected from them.' One that was then moving to Pennsylvania (meaning one that was then removing from New York with intent to reside at Pennsylvania), to which place it is reported that several considerable men are removing (from New York meaning), expressed in terms very moving much concern for the circumstances of New York (the bad circumstances of the Province and people of New York meaning), and seemed to think them very much owing to the influence that some men (whom he called tools) had in the administration (meaning the administration of government of the said Province of New York). He said he was now going from them, and was not to be hurt by any measures they should take, but could not help having some concern for the welfare of his countrymen, and should be glad to hear that the Assembly (meaning the General Assembly of the Province of New York) would exert themselves as became them by showing that they have the interest of their country more at heart than the gratification of any private view of any of their members, or being at all affected by the smiles or frowns of a governor (His Excellency the said Governor meaning); both of which ought equally to be despised when the interest of their country is at stake.

"'You,' says he, 'complain of the lawyers, but I think the law itself is at an end. We (the people of the Province of New York meaning) see men's deeds destroyed, judges arbitrarily displaced, new courts erected without consent of the legislature (within the Province of New York meaning) by which it seems to me trial by jury is taken away when a governor pleases (His Excellency the said Governor meaning), and men of known estates denied their votes contrary to the received practice, the best expositor of any law. Who is there then in that Province (meaning the Province of New York) that can call anything his own, or enjoy any liberty, longer than those in the administration (meaning the administration of government of the said Province of New York) will condescend to let them do it? For which reason I have left it, as I believe more will.'

"These words are to the great disturbance of the peace of the said Province of New York, to the great scandal of the king, of His Excellency the Governor, and of all others concerned in the administration of the government of the Province, and against the peace of the king, his crown, and his dignity.

"Whereupon the said Attorney General of the king prays the advisement of the Court here, in the premises, and the due process of law against the said John Peter Zenger.

"To this information the defendant has pleaded 'Not guilty,' but we are ready to prove [Zenger's guilt]."

At this point, Zenger's attorney rose and made an initial statement. Chambers did not provide Zenger with his notes, so the printer was unable to set down his argument and response to the attorney general. This was hardly an oversight on Chambers's part — his appointment was by the court itself, and he was obviously hopeful of subsequent reward — which he got. But, as a good lawyer should, he expounded on the nature of a libel and maintained that great allowances ought to be made for what men speak or write, that in all libels some particular persons must be so clearly pointed out that no doubt remains about who is meant and that he believed the prosecuting attorney would fail to prove this point and, therefore, desired him to proceed to an examination of his witnesses.

Then must have occurred one of the most dramatic real courtroom moments of American history: Andrew Hamilton, sixty years of age, with so massive a legal reputation as to dwarf the presiding jurists, rose to announce his purpose in attending these proceedings. He got right to the point in his first words:

MR. HAMILTON. "May it please Your Honor, I am concerned in this cause on the part of Mr. Zenger, the defendant. The information against my client was sent me a few days before I left home, with some instructions to let me know how far I might rely upon the truth of those parts of the papers set forth in the information, and which are said to be libelous.

"Although I am perfectly of the opinion with the gentleman who has just now spoken on the same side with me, as to the common course of proceedings meant in putting Mr. Attorney upon proving that my client printed and published those papers mentioned in the information yet I cannot think it proper for me (without doing violence to my own principles) to deny the publication of a complaint, which I think is the right of every freeborn subject to make when the matters so published can be supported with truth.

"Therefore I shall save Mr. Attorney the trouble of examining his witnesses to that point. I do (for my client) confess[4] that he both printed and published the two newspapers set forth in the information — and I hope that in so doing he has committed no crime."

MR. ATTORNEY. "Then if Your Honor pleases, since Mr. Hamilton has confessed the fact, I think our witnesses may be discharged. We have no further occasion for them."

MR. HAMILTON. "If you brought them here only to prove the printing and publishing of these newspapers, we have acknowledged that, and shall abide by it."

Here Zenger's journeyman associate and two of his sons, along with several others who had been subpoenaed by the prosecution in order to establish the fact of Zenger's having authorized and supervised the printing were allowed to go home, and there was silence in the court for some time. Finally, DeLancey spoke.

MR. CHIEF JUSTICE. "Well, Mr. Attorney, will you proceed?"

MR. ATTORNEY. "Indeed, Sir, as Mr. Hamilton has confessed the printing and publishing of these libels, I think the Jury must find a verdict for the king. For supposing they were true, the law says that they are not the less libelous for that. Nay, indeed the law says their being true is an aggravation of the crime."

MR. HAMILTON. "Not so neither, Mr. Attorney. There are two words to that bargain. I hope it is not our bare printing and publishing a paper that will make it a libel. You will have something more to do before you make my client a libeler. For the words themselves must be libelous that is, false, scandalous, and seditious or else we are not guilty."

As Bradley did not see much merit in placing the written text of his argument at the disposal of Zenger and his editorial brain trust, the printer was unable to set the attorney general's words down precisely as they had been given. However, the defending lawyers did have notes on the legal texts from which the prosecutor read and on the cases that he cited along with the general scope of the argument drawn from those authorities. Thus, Zenger's *Narrative* continues by attributing the following arguments to Bradley:

> He observed upon the excellency as well as the use of government, and the great regard and reverence which had been constantly paid to it, under both the law and the Gospels. That by government we were protected in our lives, religion, and properties; and for these reasons great care had always been taken to prevent everything that might tend to scandalize magistrates and others concerned in the administration of the government, especially the supreme magistrate. And that there were many instances of very severe judgments, and of punishments, inflicted upon such as had attempted to bring the government into contempt by publishing false and scurrilous libels against it, or by speaking evil and scandalous words of men in authority, to the great disturbance of the public peace. And to support this he cited various legal texts.
>
> From these books he insisted that a libel was a malicious defamation of any person, expressed either in printing or writing, signs or pictures, to asperse the reputation of one that is alive, or the memory of one that is dead. If he is a private man, the libeler deserves a severe punishment, but if it is against a magistrate or other public person, it is a greater offense. For this concerns not only the breach of the peace but the scandal of the government. What greater scandal of government can there be than to have corrupt or wicked magistrates appointed by the king to govern his subjects? A greater imputation to the state there cannot be than to suffer such corrupt men to Sit in the sacred seat of justice, or to have any meddling in or concerning the administration of justice.
>
> From the same books Mr. Attorney insisted that whether the person defamed is a private man or a magistrate, whether living or dead, whether the libel is true or false, or if the party against whom it is made is of good or evil fame, it is nevertheless a libel. For in a settled state of government the party grieved ought to complain, for every injury done him, in the ordinary course of the law. And as to its publication, the law had taken so great care of men's reputations that if one maliciously repeats it, or sings it in the presence of

another, or delivers the libel or a copy of it over to scandalize the party, he is to be punished as a publisher of a libel.

He said it was likewise evident that libeling was an offense against the law of God. Acts 23:5: Then said Paul, "I wist not, brethren, that he was the high priest; for it is written Thou shalt not speak evil of the ruler of thy people." II Peter 2:10: "Despise government. Presumptuous are they, selfwilled, they are not afraid to speak evil of dignities."

He then insisted that it was clear, by the laws of God and man, that it was a very great offense to speak evil of, or to revile, those in authority over us. And that Mr. Zenger had offended in a most notorious and gross manner, in scandalizing His Excellency our governor, who is the king's immediate representative and the supreme magistrate of this Province. For can there be anything more scandalous said of a governor than what is published in those papers? Nay, not only the Governor but both the Council and the Assembly are scandalized. For there it is plainly said that "as matters now stand, their liberties and properties are precarious, and that slavery is like to be entailed on them and their posterity." And then again Mr. Zenger says, "The Assembly ought to despise the smiles or frowns of a governor; that he thinks the law is at an end; that we see men's deeds destroyed, judges arbitrarily displaced, new courts erected without consent of the legislature; that it seems that trials by jury are taken away when a governor pleases; and that none can call anything his own longer than those in the administration will condescend to let him do it."

Mr. Attorney added that he did not know what could be said in defense of a man that had so notoriously scandalized the Governor and the principal magistrates and officers of the government by charging them with depriving the people of their rights and liberties, taking away trial by jury, and, in short, putting an end to the law itself. If this was not a libel, he said, he did not know what was one. Such persons as will take those liberties with governors and magistrates he thought ought to suffer for stirring up sedition and discontent among the people.

He concluded by saying that the government had been very much traduced and exposed by Mr. Zenger before he was taken notice of; that at last it was the opinion of the Governor and the Council that he ought not to be suffered to go on to disturb the peace of the government by publishing such libels against the Governor and the chief persons in the government; and therefore they had directed this prosecution to put a stop to this scandalous and wicked practice of libeling and defaming His Majesty's government and disturbing His Majesty's peace.

Mr. Chambers then summed up to the jury, observing with great strength of reason on Mr. Attorney's defect of proof that the papers in the information were false, malicious, or seditious, which it was incumbent on him to prove to the jury, and without which they could not on their oaths say that they were so as charged.

It is a commonplace of legal thinking that in a jury trial it is one thing to have the facts on your side, another thing to have the law on your side, a third thing to have the judge on your side, but best of all is to have a respected lawyer. Zenger clearly had the last as well as the first — and his strong points were far weightier than his weaknesses with the jury.

IX
Pleading the Negative

The words of North America's most skilled courtroom lawyer and political debater now began to have their impact. Hamilton had a generation's more experience with court procedures than the presiding justice and nearly as many years more than both his associate and the prosecutor. His skill and his credentials were unmatched in any of the colonies. More and more, it will be seen, he directed his arguments not at the judges, who—serving at the "pleasure" of the governor—clearly were not about to be dissuaded from whatever he wished, but towards the men of the jury, freeholders and taxpayers of New York.

MR. HAMILTON. "May it please Your Honor, I agree with Mr. Attorney that government is a sacred thing, but I differ widely from him when he would insinuate that the just complaints of a number of men who suffer under a bad administration is libeling that administration. Had I believed that to be law, I should not have given the Court the trouble of hearing anything that I could say in this cause.

"I own that when I read the information I had not the art to find out, without the help of Mr. Attorney's innuendos, that the Governor was the person meant in every period of that newspaper. I was inclined to believe that they were written by some who, from an extraordinary zeal for liberty, had misconstrued the conduct of some persons in authority into crimes; and that Mr. Attorney, out of his too great zeal for power, had exhibited this information to correct the indiscretion of my client, and at the same time to show his superiors the great concern he had lest they should be treated with any undue freedom.

"But from what Mr. Attorney has just now said, to wit, that this prosecution was directed by the Governor and the Council, and from the extraordinary appearance of people of all conditions, which I observe in Court upon this occasion, I have reason to think that those in the administration have by this prosecution something more in view, and that the people believe they have a good deal . more at stake, than I apprehended. Therefore, as it is become my duty to be both plain and particular in this cause, I beg leave to bespeak the patience of the Court."

Now Hamilton began to play on the lingering nightmare of all freeholders — the proceedings formerly held in the Star Chamber of Westminster Palace. While the name of the room derives merely from some stars that were painted on the ceiling of the king's council room, the room's name had taken on sinister implications of torture, secrecy and mysterious deaths. The Star Chamber's judicial uses had evolved into instruments of illegality under the Tudor and Stuart regimes. While most of its proceedings were aimed at suspect members of the nobility, the Star Chamber's denial of self-defense and jury trial were so well-known that there was great rejoicing when the "Long Parliament" abolished its judicial functions in 1641. It's memory, however, lingered on and Hamilton made the most of it.

> "I was in hopes as that terrible Court where those dreadful judgments were given, and that law established, which Mr. Attorney has produced for authorities to support this cause, was long ago laid aside as the most dangerous Court to the liberties of the people of England that ever was known in that kingdom — that Mr. Attorney, knowing this, would not have attempted to set up a star chamber here, nor to make their judgments a precedent to us. For it is well known that what would have been judged treason in those days for a man to speak, has since not only been practiced as lawful, but the contrary doctrine has been held to be law."

Hamilton turned then to some specifics, drawing first on the case of Thomas Brewster, one of the many printers prosecuted under the various licensing laws during the reign of Charles II. This man had printed a defense of those who had been party to the execution of Charles I, and was convicted in 1663.

> "In Brewster's case for printing that subjects might defend their rights and liberties by arms in case the king should go about to destroy them, he was told by the Chief Justice that it was a great mercy he was not proceeded against for his life; for to say the king could be resisted by arms in any case whatsoever was express treason. And yet we see since that time, that Doctor Sacheverell was sentenced in the highest court in Great Britain for saying that such a

resistance was not lawful. Besides, as times have made very great changes in the laws of England, so in my opinion there is good reason that [other] places should do so too.

"Is it not surprising to see a subject, upon receiving a commission from the king to be a governor of a Colony in America, immediately imagining himself to be vested with all the prerogatives belonging to the sacred person of his princes? And, which is yet more astonishing, to see that a people can be so wild as to allow of and acknowledge those prerogatives and exemptions, even to their own destruction? Is it so hard a matter to distinguish between the majesty of our sovereign and the power of a governor of The Plantations?[1] Is not this making very free with our prince, to apply that regard, obedience, and allegiance to a subject, which is due only to our sovereign?

"And yet in all the cases which Mr. Attorney has cited to show the duty and obedience we owe to the supreme magistrate, it is the king that is there meant and understood, although Mr. Attorney is pleased to urge them as authorities to prove the heinousness of Mr. Zenger's offense against the Governor of New York. The several Plantations are compared to so many large corporations, and perhaps not improperly.[2] Can anyone give an instance that the head of a corporation ever put in a claim to the sacred rights of majesty? Let us not, while we are pretending to pay a great regard to our prince and his peace, make bold to transfer that allegiance to a subject which we owe to our king only.

"What strange doctrine is it to press everything for law here which is so in England? I believe we should not think it a favor, at present at least, to establish this practice. In England so great a regard and reverence is had to the judges that if any man strikes another in Westminster Hall while the judges are sitting, he shall lose his right hand and forfeit his land and goods for so doing. Although the judges here claim all the powers and authorities within this government that a Court of King's Bench has in England, yet I believe Mr. Attorney will scarcely say that such a punishment could be legally inflicted on a man for committing such an offense in the presence of the judges sitting in any court within the Province of New York. The reason is obvious. A quarrel or riot in New York cannot possibly be attended with those dangerous consequences that it might in Westminster Hall; nor, I hope, will it be alleged that any misbehavior to a governor in The Plantations will, or ought to be, judged of or punished as a like undutifulness would be to our sovereign.

"From all of which, I hope Mr. Attorney will not think it proper to apply his law cases, to support the cause of his governor, which have only been judged where the king's safety or honor was concerned.

"It will not be denied that a freeholder in the Province of New York has as good a right to the sole and separate use of his lands as a freeholder in England, who has a right to bring an action of trespass against his neighbor for suffering his horse or cow to come and feed upon his land or eat his corn, whether enclosed or not. Yet I believe it would be looked upon as a strange attempt for one man here to bring an action against another whose cattle and horses feed upon his grounds that are not enclosed, or indeed for eating and treading down his corn, if that were not enclosed.

"Numberless are the instances of this kind that might be given to show that what is good law at one time and in one place is not so at another time and in another place. So that I think the law seems to expect that in these parts of the world men should take care, by a good fence, to preserve their property from the injury of unruly beasts. And perhaps there may be a good reason why men should take the same care to make an honest and upright conduct a fence and security against the injury of unruly tongues."

MR. ATTORNEY. "I don't know what the gentleman means by comparing cases of freeholders in England with freeholders here. What has this case to do with actions of trespass or men's fencing their ground? The case before the Court is whether Mr. Zenger is guilty of libeling His Excellency the Governor of New York, and indeed the whole administration of the government. Mr. Hamilton has confessed the printing and publishing, and I think nothing is plainer than that the words in the information are 'scandalous, and tend to sedition, and to disquiet the minds of the people of this Province.' If such papers are not libels, I think it may be said that there can be no such thing as a libel."

MR. HAMILTON. "May it please Your Honor, I cannot agree with Mr. Attorney. For although I freely acknowledge that there are such things as libels, yet I must insist at the same time that what my client is charged with is not a libel. And I observed just now that Mr. Attorney, in defining a libel, made use of the words 'scandalous, seditious, and tend to disquiet the people.' But, whether with design or not I will not say, he omitted the word 'false.'"

MR. ATTORNEY. "I think that I did not omit the word 'false.' But it has been said already that it may be a libel notwithstanding that it may be true."

MR. HAMILTON. "In this I must still differ with Mr. Attorney. For I depend upon it that we are to be tried upon this information now before the Court and the jury, and to which we have pleaded 'Not guilty.' By it we are charged with printing and publishing 'a

certain false, malicious, seditious, and scandalous libel.' This word
'false' must have some meaning, or else how came it there? I hope
Mr. Attorney will not say he put it there by chance, and I am of the
opinion that his information would not be good without it. But to
show that it is the principal thing which, in my opinion, makes a
libel, suppose that the information had been for printing and publishing a certain true libel, would that be the same thing? Or could
Mr. Attorney support such an information by any precedent in the
English law? No, the falsehood makes the scandal, and both make
the libel. And to show the Court that I am in good earnest, and to
save the Court's time and Mr. Attorney's trouble, I will agree that
if he can prove the facts charged upon us to be false, I shall own them
to be scandalous, seditious, and a libel. So the work seems now to
be pretty much shortened, and Mr. Attorney has now only to prove
the words false in order to make us guilty."

Here Hamilton had scored a solid point with the jury. But Bradley
very wisely opted to ignore the body blow to his case and switched his
line of attack.

MR. ATTORNEY. "We have nothing to prove. You have confessed the printing and publishing. But if it were necessary, as I
insist it is not, how can we prove a negative? I hope some regard
will be had to the authorities that have been produced, and that
supposing all the words to be true, yet that will not help them. Chief
Justice Holt, in his charge to the jury in the case of Tutchin, made
no distinction whether Tutchin's papers were true or false; and as
Chief Justice Holt has made no distinction in that case, so none
ought to be made here; nor can it be shown that, in all that case,
there was any question made about their being false or true."[3]
MR. HAMILTON. "I did expect to hear that a negative cannot be
proved. But everybody knows there are many exceptions to that
general rule. For if a man is charged with killing another, or steal-
ing his neighbor's horse, if he is innocent in the one case he may
prove the man said to be killed to be really alive, and the horse said
to be stolen never to have been out of his master's stable, etc. And
this, I think, is proving a negative.
"But we will save Mr. Attorney the trouble of proving a negative,
take the onus probandi [burden of proof] on ourselves, and prove
those very papers that are called libels to be true."
MR. CHIEF JUSTICE. "You cannot be admitted, Mr. Hamilton,
to give the truth of a libel in evidence. A libel is not to be justified;
for it is nevertheless a libel that it is true."

MR. HAMILTON. "I am sorry the Court has so soon resolved upon that piece of law. I expected first to have been heard to that point. I have not, in all my reading, met with an authority that says we cannot be admitted to give the truth in evidence upon an information for libel."

MR. CHIEF JUSTICE. "The law is clear that you cannot justify a libel."

MR. HAMILTON. "I own that, may it please Your Honor, to be so. But, with submission, I understand the word 'justify' there to be a justification by plea, as it is in the case upon an indictment for murder or an assault and battery. There the prisoner cannot justify, but pleads 'Not guilty.' Yet it will not be denied but he may be, and always is, admitted to give the truth of the fact, or any other matter, in evidence, which goes to his acquittal. As in murder he may prove that it was in defense of his life, his house, etc.; and in assault and battery he may give in evidence that the other party struck first: and in both cases he will be acquitted. In this sense I understand the word 'justify' when applied to the case before the Court."

MR. CHIEF JUSTICE. "I pray, show that you can give the truth of a libel in evidence."

Justice DeLancey's point was thus discussed: was there precedent in English law to prove that a person accused of libel had been allowed to defend himself on the ground that the statement was true?

MR. HAMILTON. "How shall it be known whether the words are libelous, that is, true or false, but by admitting us to prove them true, since Mr. Attorney will not undertake to prove them false? Besides, is it not against common sense that a man should be punished in the same degree for a true libel, if any such thing could be, as for a false one? I know it is said that truth makes a libel the more provoking, and therefore the offense is greater, and consequently the judgment should be the heavier. Well, suppose it were so, and let us agree for once that truth is a greater sin than falsehood. Yet, as the offenses are not equal, and as the punishment is arbitrary, that is, according as the judges in their discretion shall direct to be inflicted, is it not absolutely necessary that they should know whether the libel is true or false, that they may by that means be able to proportion the punishment?

"For would it not be a sad case if the judges, for want of a due information, should chance to give as severe a judgement against a man for writing or publishing a lie, as for writing or publishing a truth? And yet this, with submission, as monstrous and ridiculous as it may seem to be, is the natural consequence of Mr. Attorney's doctrine that truth makes a worse libel than falsehood, and must follow from his not proving our papers to be false, or not suffering us to prove them to be true.

"In the case of Tutchin, which seems to be Mr. Attorney's chief authority, that case is against him; for Tutchin was, at his trial, put upon showing the truth of his papers; but he did not. At least the prisoner was asked by the king's counsel whether he would say that they were true. And as he never pretended that they were true, the Chief Justice was not to say so.

"But the point will be clearer on our side from Fuller's case.[4] Here you see is a scandalous and infamous charge against the late king; here is a charge no less than high treason, against the men in public trust, for receiving money of the French king, then in actual war with the crown of Great Britain; and yet the Court were far from bearing him down with that star chamber doctrine, to wit, that it was no matter whether what he said was true or false. No, on the contrary, Lord Chief Justice Holt asks Fuller, 'Can you make it appear that they are true? Have you any witnesses? You might have had subpoenas for your witnesses against this day. If you take it upon you to write such things as you are charged with, it lies upon you to prove them true, at your peril. If you have any witnesses, I will hear them. How came you to write those books which are not true? If you have any witnesses, produce them. If you can offer any matter to prove what you wrote, let us hear it.' Thus said, and thus did, that great man, Lord Chief Justice Holt, upon a trial of the like kind with ours; and the rule laid down by him in this case is that he who will take upon him to write things, it lies upon him to prove them, at his peril. Now, sir, we have acknowledged the printing and publishing of those papers set forth in the information and, with the leave of the Court, agreeable to the rule laid down by Chief Justice Holt, we are ready to prove them to be true, at our peril."

MR. CHIEF JUSTICE. "Let me see the book."

Hamilton offered DeLancey the text of Holt's decision relative to Fuller. While the two justices conferred privately for a considerable time, everyone in the courtroom was silent.

MR. CHIEF JUSTICE. "Mr. Attorney, you have heard what Mr. Hamilton has said, and the cases he has cited, for having his witnesses examined to prove the truth of the several facts contained in the papers set forth in the information. What do you say to it?"

MR. ATTORNEY. "The law, in my opinion, is very clear. They

cannot be admitted to justify a libel, for by the authorities I have already read to the Court it is not the less a libel because it is true. I think I need not trouble the Court over again. The thing seems to be very plain, and I submit it to the Court."

MR. CHIEF JUSTICE. "Mr. Hamilton, the Court is of the opinion that you ought not to be permitted to prove the facts in the papers. These are the words of the book, 'It is far from being a justification of a libel that the contents thereof are true, or that the person upon whom it is made had a bad reputation, since the greater appearance there is of truth in any malicious invective, so much the more provoking it is.'"

MR. HAMILTON. "These are Star Chamber cases, and I was in hopes that practice had been dead with the court."

MR. CHIEF JUSTICE. "Mr. Hamilton, the Court have delivered their opinion, and we expect that you will use us with good manners. You are not to be permitted to argue against the opinion of the Court."

MR. HAMILTON. "With submission, I have seen the practice in very great courts, and never heard it deemed unmannerly to—"

MR. CHIEF JUSTICE. "After the Court have declared their opinion, it is not good manners to insist upon a point in which you are overruled."

MR. HAMILTON. "I will say no more at this time. The Court, I see, is against us in this point—and that I hope I may be allowed to say."

MR. CHIEF JUSTICE. "Use the Court with good manners and you shall be allowed all the liberty you can reasonably desire."

MR. HAMILTON. "I thank Your Honor. Then, Gentlemen of the Jury, it is to you that we must now appeal for witnesses to the truth of the facts we have offered, and are denied the liberty to prove. Let it not seem strange that I apply myself to you in this manner. I am warranted by both law and reason.

"The law supposes you to be summoned out of the neighborhood where the fact is alleged to be committed; and the reason of your being taken out of the neighborhood is because you are supposed to have the best knowledge of the fact that is to be tried. Were you to find a verdict against my client, you must take it upon you to say that the papers referred to in the information, and which we acknowledge we printed and published, are false, scandalous, and seditious.

"But of this I can have no apprehension. You are citizens of New York. You are really what the law supposes you to be, honest and lawful men; and according to my brief, the facts which we offer to prove were not committed in a corner. They are notoriously known to be true. Therefore in your justice lies our safety. And as we are denied the liberty of giving evidence to prove the truth of what we have published, I will beg leave to lay it down as a standing rule in such cases that the suppressing of evidence ought always to be taken for the strongest evidence; and I hope it will have that weight with you.

"But since we are not admitted to examine our witnesses, I will endeavor to shorten the dispute with Mr. Attorney, and to that end I desire he would favor us with some standard definition of a libel by which it may be certainly known whether a writing be a libel, yes or no."

MR. ATTORNEY. "The books, I think, have given a very full definition of libel."

MR. HAMILTON. "Ay, Mr. Attorney, but what standard rule have the books laid down by which we can certainly know whether the words or signs are malicious? Whether they are defamatory? Whether they tend to the breach of the peace, and are a sufficient ground to provoke a man, his family, or his friends to acts of revenge: especially the ironical sort of words? What rule have you to know when I write ironically? I think it would be hard when I say, 'Such a man is a very worthy honest gentleman, and of fine understanding,' that therefore I mean, 'He is a knave or a fool.'"

MR. ATTORNEY. "I think the books are very full. It is said in Hawkins just now read, 'Such scandal as is expressed in a scoffing and ironical manner makes a writing as properly a libel as that which is expressed in direct terms.' I think nothing can be plainer or more full than these words."

MR. HAMILTON. "I agree the words are very plain, and I shall not scruple to allow (when we are agreed that the words are false and scandalous, and were spoken in an ironical and scoffing manner) that they are really libelous. But here still occurs the uncertainty which makes the difficulty to know what words are scandalous, and what are not. For you say that they may be scandalous, whether true or false.

"Besides, how shall we know whether the words were spoken in a scoffing and ironical manner, or seriously? Or how can you know whether the man did not think as he wrote? For by your rule, if he did, it is no irony, and consequently no libel.

"But under favor, Mr. Attorney, I think the same book, and under the same section, will show us the only rule by which all these things are to be known. The words are these, 'which kind of writing is as well understood to mean only to upbraid the parties with the want of these qualities as if they had directly and expressly done so.' Here it is plain that the words are scandalous, scoffing, and ironical only as they are understood. I know no rule laid down in the books but this, I mean, as the words are understood."

MR. CHIEF JUSTICE. "Mr. Hamilton, do you think it so hard to know when words are ironical or spoken in a scoffing manner?"

MR. HAMILTON. "I own it may be known. But I insist that the only rule by which to know is — as I do or can understand them. I have no other rule to go by but as I understand them."

MR. CHIEF JUSTICE. "That is certain. All words are libelous or not as they are understood. Those who are to judge of the words must judge whether they are scandalous, or ironical, or tend to the breach of the peace, or are seditious. There can be no doubt of it."

MR. HAMILTON. "I thank Your Honor. I am glad to find the Court of this opinion. Then it follows that these twelve men must understand the words in the information to be scandalous — that is to say, false. For I think it is not pretended they are of the ironical sort. And [only] when they understand the words to be so, they will say that we are guilty of publishing a false libel, and not otherwise."

MR. CHIEF JUSTICE. "No, Mr. Hamilton, the jury may find that Zenger printed and published those papers, and leave it to the Court to judge whether they are libelous. You know this is very common. It is in the nature of a special verdict, where the jury leave the matter of the law to the court."

MR. HAMILTON. "I know, may it please Your Honor, the jury may do so. But I do likewise know that they may do otherwise. I know that they have the right beyond all dispute to determine both the law and the fact; and where they do not doubt of the law, they ought to do so. Leaving it to judgment of the court whether the words are libelous or not in effect renders juries useless (to say no worse) in many cases. But this I shall have occasion to speak to by and by.

"Although I own it to be base and unworthy to scandalize any man, yet I think it is even more villainous to scandalize a person of public character. I will go so far into Mr. Attorney's doctrine as to agree that if the faults, mistakes, nay even the vices of such a person be private and personal, and do not affect the peace of the public, or the liberty or property of our neighbor, it is unmanly and unmannerly to expose them either by word or writing. But when a ruler of a people brings his personal failings, but much more his vices, into his administration, and the people find themselves affected by them either in their liberties or properties, that will alter the case mightily; and all the things that are said in favor of rulers and of dignitaries, and upon the side of power, will not be able to stop people's mouths when they feel themselves oppressed. I mean, in a free government."

MR. ATTORNEY. "Pray, Mr. Hamilton, have a care what you say, don't go too far. I don't like those liberties."

MR. HAMILTON. "Surely, Mr. Attorney, you won't make any applications. All men agree that we are governed by the best of kings, and I cannot see the meaning of Mr. Attorney's caution. My well-known principles, and the sense I have of the blessings we enjoy under His Majesty, make it impossible for me to err, and I hope even to be suspected, in that point of duty to my king."

With this parting shot Hamilton resumed his attention towards convincing the people of New York, as represented by the freeholders on the jury.

X
Pleading the Truth

In his lengthy summary to the jury, Andrew Hamilton dwelt little on precedents or the law itself, which was decidedly vague anyway, but very much upon principles of elementary justice with which he was sure his listeners could relate. In so doing, he was also able to establish the principle that for any statement to be a libel, it had to be both false and injurious. This was a point of law that relative to news media remained fundamentally unchanged for 237 years — even in its subsequent alteration, it was only to be liberalized.

"May it please Your Honor, I was saying that notwithstanding all the duty and reverence claimed by Mr. Attorney to men in authority, they are not exempt from observing the rules of common justice either in their private or public capacities. The laws of our mother country know no exemptions. It is true that men in power are harder to be come at for wrongs they do either to a private person or to the public, especially a governor in The Plantations, where they insist upon an exemption from answering complaints of any kind in their own government. We are indeed told, and it is true, that they are obliged to answer a suit in the king's courts at Westminster for a wrong done to any person here. But do we not know how impracticable this is to most men among us, to leave their families, who depend upon their labor and care for their livelihood, and carry evidence to Britain, and at a great, nay, a far greater expense than almost any of us are able to bear, only to prosecute a governor for an injury done here?

"But when the oppression is general, there is no remedy even that way. No, our Constitution has — blessed be God — given us an opportunity, if not to have such wrongs redressed, yet by our prudence and resolution we may in a great measure prevent the committing of such wrongs by making a governor sensible that it is in his interest to be just to those under his care. For such is the sense that men in general — I mean free men — have of common justice, that when they come to know that a chief magistrate abuses the power with which he is trusted for the good of the people, and is attempting to turn that very power against the innocent, whether of high or low degree, I say that mankind in general seldom fail to interpose, and, as far as they can, prevent the destruction of their fellow subjects.

"And has it not often been seen — I hope it will always be seen — that when the representatives of a free people are by just representations or remonstrances made sensible of the sufferings of their fellow subjects, by the abuse of power in the hands of a governor, that they have declared (and loudly too) that they were not obliged by any law to support a governor who goes about to destroy a Province or Colony, or their privileges, which by His Majesty he was appointed, and by the law he is bound, to protect and encourage? But I pray that it may be considered — of what use is this mighty privilege if every man that suffers is silent? And if a man must be taken up as a libeler for telling his sufferings to his neighbor?

"I know that it may be answered, 'Have you not a legislature? Have you not a House of Representatives to whom you may complain?' To this I answer, 'We have.' But what then? Is an Assembly to be troubled with every injury done by a governor? Or are they to hear of nothing but what those in the administration will please to tell them? And what sort of trial must a man have? How is he to be remedied, especially if the case were, as I have known to happen in America in my time, that a governor who has places — I will not say pensions, for I believe they seldom give that to another which they can take to themselves — to bestow can keep the same Assembly, after he has modeled them so as to get a majority of the House in his interest, for near twice seven years together? I pray, what redress is to be expected for an honest man who makes his complaint against a governor to an Assembly who may properly enough be said to be made by the same governor against whom the complaint is made? The thing answers itself.

"No, it is natural, it is a privilege, I will go farther, it is a right, which all free men claim, that they are entitled to complain when they are hurt. They have a right publicly to remonstrate against the abuses of power in the strongest terms, to put their neighbors upon their guard against the craft or open violence of men in authority, and to assert with courage the sense they have of the blessings of liberty, the value they put upon it, and their resolution at all hazards to preserve it as one of the greatest blessings heaven can bestow.

"When a House of Assembly composed of honest freemen sees the general bent of the people's inclination, that is it which must and will, I am sure it ought to, weigh with a legislature in spite of all the craft, caressing, and cajoling made use of by a governor to divert them from harkening to the voice of their country. As we all very well understand the true reason why gentlemen take so much pains and make such great interest to be appointed governors, so is the design of their appointment not less manifest. We know His Majesty's gracious intentions toward his subjects. He desires no more than that his people in The Plantations should be kept up to their duty and allegiance to the crown of Great Britain, that peace may be preserved among them, and justice impartially administered; so that we may be governed so as to render us useful to our mother country by encouraging us to make and raise such commodities as may be useful to Great Britain.

"But will anyone say that all or any of these good ends are to be effected by a governor's setting his people together by the ears, and by the assistance of one part of the people to plague and plunder the other? The commission that governors bear while they execute the powers given them according to the intent of the royal grantor requires and deserves very great reverence and submission. But when a governor departs from the duty enjoined on him by his sovereign, and acts as if he were less accountable than the royal hand that gave him all that power and honor that he is possessed of, this sets people upon examining and inquiring into the power, authority, and duty of such a magistrate, and to comparing those with his conduct. And just as far as they find he exceeds the bounds of his authority, or falls short in doing impartial justice to the people under his administration, so far they very often, in return, come short in their duty to such a governor.

"For power alone will not make a man beloved, and I have heard it observed that the man who was neither good nor wise before his being made a governor never mended upon his preferment, but has been generally observed to be worse. For men who are not imbued with wisdom and virtue can only be kept in bounds by the law; and by how much the further they think themselves out of the reach of the law, by so much the more wicked and cruel men are. I wish there were no instances of the kind at this day.

"Wherever this happens to be the case of a governor, unhappy are the people under his administration, and in the end he will find himself so too, for the people will neither love him nor support him.

"I make no doubt but there are those here who are zealously concerned for the success of this prosecution, and yet I hope they are not many; and even some of those, I am persuaded, when they consider to what lengths such prosecutions may be carried, and how deeply the liberties of the people may be affected by such means, will not all abide by their present sentiments. I say 'not all,' for the man who from an intimacy and acquaintance with a governor has conceived a personal regard for him, the man who has felt none of the strokes of his power, the man who believes that a governor has a regard for him and confides in him it is natural for such men to wish well to the affairs of such a governor. And as they may be men of honor and generosity, may, and no doubt will, wish him success so far as the rights and privileges of their fellow citizens are not affected. But as men of honor I can apprehend nothing from them. They will never exceed that point.

"There are others that are under stronger obligations, and those are such as are in some sort engaged in support of the governor's cause by their own or their relations' dependence on his favor for some post or preferment. Such men have what is commonly called duty and gratitude to influence their inclinations and oblige them to go his lengths. I know men's interests are very near to them, and they will do much rather than forgo the favor of a governor and a livelihood at the same time. But I can with very just grounds hope, even from those men, whom I will suppose to be men of honor and conscience too, that when they see the liberty of their country in danger, either by their concurrence or even by their silence, they will like Englishmen, and like themselves, freely make a sacrifice of any preferment or favor rather than be accessory to destroying the liberties of their country and entailing slavery upon their posterity.

"There are indeed another set of men, of whom I have no hopes. I mean such who lay aside all other considerations and are ready to join with power in any shape, and with any man or sort of men by whose means or interest they may be assisted to gratify their malice and envy against those whom they have been pleased to hate; and that for no other reason than because they are men of ability and integrity, or at least are possessed of some valuable qualities far superior to their own. But as envy is the sin of the Devil, and therefore very hard, if at all, to be repented of, I will believe there are but few of this detestable and worthless sort of men, nor will their opinions or inclinations have any influence upon this trial.

"But to proceed. I beg leave to insist that the right of complaining or remonstrating is natural; that the restraint upon this natural right is the law only; and that those restraints can only extend to what is false. For as it is truth alone that can excuse or justify any man for complaining of a bad administration, I as frankly agree that nothing ought to excuse a man who raises a false charge or accusation even against a private person, and that no manner of allowance ought to be made to him who does so against a public magistrate.

"Truth ought to govern the whole affair of libels. And yet the party accused runs risk enough even then; for if he fails in proving every title of what he has written, and to the satisfaction of the court and jury too, he may find to his cost that when the prosecution is set on foot by men in power it seldom wants friends to favor it.

"From thence (it is said) has arisen the great diversity of opinions among judges about what words were or were not scandalous or libelous. I believe it will be granted that there is not greater uncertainty in any part of the law than about words of scandal. It would be misspending of the Court's time to mention the cases. They may be said to be numberless. Therefore the utmost care ought to be taken in following precedents; and the times when the judgments were given, which are quoted for authorities in the case of libels, are much to be regarded.

"I think it will be agreed that ever since the time of the Star Chamber, where the most arbitrary judgments and opinions were given that ever an Englishman heard of, at least in his own country; I say, prosecutions for libel since the time of that arbitrary Court, and until the Glorious Revolution, have generally been set on foot at the instance of the crown or its ministers. And it is no small reproach to the law that these prosecutions were too often and too much countenanced by the judges, who held their places 'at pleasure,' a disagreeable tenure to any officer, but a dangerous one in the case of a judge. Yet I cannot think it unwarrantable to show the unhappy influence that a sovereign has sometimes had, not only upon judges, but even upon parliaments themselves.

"It has already been shown how the judges differed in their opinions about the nature of a libel in the case of the Seven Bishops.[1]

"There you see three judges of one opinion, that is, of a wrong opinion in the judgment of the best men in England, and one judge of a right opinion. How unhappy might it have been for all of us at this day if that jury had understood the words in that information as the Court did? Or if they had left it to the Court to judge whether the petition of the Bishops was or was not a libel? No, they took upon them[selves] — to their immortal honor — to determine both law and fact, and to understand the petition of the Bishops to be no libel, that is, to contain no falsehood or sedition; and therefore found them not guilty.

"If then upon the whole there is so great an uncertainty among judges — learned and great men — in matters of this kind, if power has had so great an influence on judges, how cautious ought we to be in determining by their judgments especially in The Plantations, and in the case of libels?

"There is heresy in law as well as in religion, and both have changed very much. We well know that it is not two centuries ago that a man would have been burned as a heretic for owning such opinions in matters of religion as are publicly written and printed at this day. They were fallible men, it seems, and we take the liberty not only to differ from them in religious opinions, but to condemn them and their opinions too. I must presume that in taking these freedoms in thinking and speaking about matters of faith or religion, we are in the right; for although it is said that there are very great liberties of this kind taken in New York, yet I have heard of no information preferred by Mr. Attorney for any offenses of this sort. From which I think it is pretty clear that in New York a man may make very free with his God, but he must take a special care what he says of his governor.

"It is agreed upon by all men that this is a reign of liberty. While men keep within the bounds of truth I hope they may with safety both speak and write their sentiments of the conduct of men in power, I mean of that part of their conduct only which affects the liberty or property of the people under their administration. Were this to be denied, then the next step may make them slaves; for what notions can be entertained of slavery beyond that of suffering the greatest injuries and oppressions without the liberty of complaining, or if they do, to be destroyed, body and estate, for so doing?

"It is said and insisted on by Mr. Attorney that government is a sacred thing; that it is to be supported and reverenced; that it is government that protects our persons and estates, prevents treasons, murders, robberies, riots, and all the train of evils that overturns kingdoms and states and ruins particular persons. And if those in the administration, especially the supreme magistrate, must have all their conduct censured by private men, government cannot subsist. This is called a licentiousness not to be tolerated. It is said that it brings the rulers of the people into contempt, and their authority not to be regarded, and so in the end the laws cannot be put into execution.

"These, I say, and such as these, are the general topics insisted upon by men in power and their advocates. But I wish it might be considered at the same time how often it has happened that the abuse of power has been the primary cause of these evils, and that it was the injustice and oppression of these great men that has commonly brought them into contempt with the people. The craft and art of such men is great, and who that is the least acquainted with history or law can be ignorant of the specious pretenses that have often been made use of by men in power to introduce arbitrary rule, and to destroy the liberties of a free people?"

At this point, according to Zenger's *Narrative,* Hamilton went back to legal history to strengthen his position on the crucial issues of the defendant's to plead truth in libel cases and the jury's right to determine both the law and the fact, that is, the jury's right to deliver a verdict of guilty or not guilty of libel, instead of leaving that culminating decision to the judges on the bench. Without naming the names, Hamilton continued by referring to the case of his old friend, Francis MacKemie, who had not only had a run-in with establishment religion when in New York, but had previously suffered from the adverse attentions of Francis Nicholson (1655–1728), who was governor of Virginia in 1704. Presumably, Hamilton felt some of his listeners would have recalled certain aspects of MacKemie's treatment in New York under Governor Edmund Hyde, Lord Cornbury.

> "This is the second information for libeling of a governor that I have known in America. The first, although it may look like a romance, yet as it is true I will beg leave to mention it.
>
> "Governor Nicholson, who happened to be offended with one of his clergy, met him one day upon the road; and as usual with him (under the protection of his commission) used the poor parson with the worst of language, and threatened to cut off his ears, slit his nose, and at last to shoot him through the head. The parson, being a reverend man, continued all this time uncovered in the heat of the sun, until he found an opportunity to fly for it. Coming to a neighbor's house, he felt himself very ill of a fever, and immediately writes for a doctor. And that his physician might the better judge of his distemper, he acquainted him with the usage he had received; concluding that the Governor was certainly mad, for that no man in his senses would have behaved in that manner.
>
> "The doctor unhappily showed the parson's letter. The Governor came to hear of it. And so an information was preferred against the poor man for saying he believed the Governor was mad. It was laid down in the information to be false, scandalous, and wicked, and written with intent to move sedition among the people, and to bring His Excellency into contempt. But by an order from the late Queen Anne there was a stop put to that prosecution, with sundry others set on foot by the same Governor against gentlemen of the greatest worth and honor in that government."

XI
Acquittal

It was by establishing the inadequacy of his opponent's premises that Hamilton would win the day. He now began to conclude his defense:

> "And may not I be allowed, after all this, to say that by a little countenance almost anything that a man writes may, with the help of that useful term of art called an innuendo, be construed to be a libel, according to Mr. Attorney's definition of it — to wit, that whether the words are spoken of a person of a public character or of a private man, whether dead or living, good or bad, true or false, all make a libel. For according to Mr. Attorney, after a man hears a writing read, or reads and repeats it, or laughs at it, they are all punishable. It is true that Mr. Attorney is so good as to allow it must be after the party knows it to be a libel, but he is not so kind as to take the man's word for it."

At this point Hamilton cited several "hypothetical" cases to show that even if what a man writes of a governor were true, proper and necessary, yet according to the doctrine argued by Attorney General Bradley they might be construed to be a libel. After the trial was over, Hamilton learned that some of these cases really had happened in Cosby's government, but declared that he had never heard of any such and that as he had meant no personal reflections, he was sorry he mentioned them. Therefore he omitted them in the material he sent to Zenger. But on that fourth of August Hamilton spared no heat in making further mincemeat of his opponent.

> "If a libel is understood in the large and unlimited sense urged by Mr. Attorney, there is scarce a writing I know that may not be called a libel, or scarce a person safe from being called to an account as a libeler. For Moses, meek as he was, libeled Cain; and who is it that has not libeled the Devil?

"For according to Mr. Attorney it is no justification to say that one has a bad name. Echard has libeled our good King William; Burnet has libeled, among others, King Charles and King James; and Rapin has libeled them all. How must a man speak or write; or what must he hear, read, or sing; or when must he laugh so as to be secure from being taken up as a libeler?

"I sincerely believe that were some persons to go through the streets of New York nowadays and read a part of the Bible, if it was not known to be such, Mr. Attorney, with the help of his innuendos, would easily turn it into a libel. As for instance Isaiah 9:16: 'The leaders of the people cause them to err; and they that are led by them are destroyed.' Should Mr. Attorney go about to make this a libel, he would read it thus: 'The leaders of the people (innuendo, the Governor and Council of New York) cause them (innuendo, the people of this Province) to err, and they (the people of this Province meaning) that are led by them (the Governor and Council meaning) are destroyed (innuendo, are deceived into the loss of their liberty), which is the worst kind of destruction.'

"Or if some person should publicly repeat, in a manner not pleasing to his betters, the 10th and 11th verses of the 56th chapter of the same book, there Mr. Attorney would have a large field to display his skill in the artful application of his innuendos. The words are: 'His watchmen are blind, they are all ignorant, ... Yea, they are greedy dogs which can never have enough.' To make them a libel there is, according to Mr. Attorney's doctrine, no more wanting but the aid of his skill in the right adapting of his innuendos. As for instance: 'His watchmen (innuendo, the Governors Council and his Assembly) are blind, they are all ignorant (innuendo, will not see the dangerous designs of His Excellency). Yea, they (the Governor and Council meaning) are greedy dogs which can never have enough (innuendo, enough of riches and power).'

"Such an instance as this seems only fit to be laughed at; but I appeal to Mr. Attorney himself whether these are not at least equally proper to be applied to His Excellency and his ministers as some of the inferences and innuendos in his information against my client. Then if Mr. Attorney is at liberty to come into court and file an information in the king's name, without leave, who is secure whom he is pleased to prosecute as a libeler?

"And give me leave to say that the mode of prosecuting by information, when a grand jury will not find a true bill, is a national grievance, and greatly inconsistent with that freedom that the subjects of England enjoy in most other cases. But if we are so unhappy as not to be able to ward off this stroke of power directly, yet let us take care not to be cheated out of our liberties by forms and appearances. Let us always be sure that the charge in the information is made out clearly even beyond a doubt; for although matters in the information may be called form upon trial, yet they may be, and often have been found to be, matters of substance upon giving Judgment.

"Gentlemen: The danger is great in proportion to the mischief that may happen through our too great credulity. A proper confidence in a court is commendable, but as the verdict, whatever it is, will be yours, you ought to refer no part of your duty to the discretion of other persons. If you should be of the opinion that there is no falsehood in Mr. Zenger's papers, you will, nay pardon me for the expression, you ought, to say so—because you do not know whether others—I mean the Court—may be of that opinion. It is your right to do so, and there is much depending upon your resolution as well as upon your integrity.

"The loss of liberty, to a generous mind, is worse than death. And yet we know that there have been those in all ages who for the sake of preferment, or some imaginary honor, have freely lent a helping hand to oppress, nay to destroy, their country.

"This brings to my mind that saying of the immortal [Marcus] Brutus when he looked upon the creatures of Caesar, who were very great men but by no means good men. 'You Romans,' said Brutus, 'if yet I may call you so, consider what you are doing. Remember that you are assisting Caesar to forge those very chains that one day he will make you yourselves wear.' This is what every man who values freedom ought to consider. He should act by judgment and not by affection or self-interest; for where those prevail, no ties of either country or kindred are regarded; as upon the other hand, the man who loves his country prefers its liberty to all other considerations, well knowing that without liberty life is a misery.

"A famous instance of this you will find in the history of another brave Roman of the same name, I mean Lucius Junius Brutus, whose story is well known, and therefore I shall mention no more of it than only to show the value he put upon the freedom of his country. After this great man, with his fellow citizens whom he had engaged in the cause, had banished Tarquin the Proud, the last king of Rome, from a throne that he ascended by inhuman murders and possessed by the most dreadful tyranny and proscriptions, and had by this means amassed incredible riches, even sufficient to bribe to his interest many of the young nobility of Rome to assist him in recovering the crown; the plot being discovered, the principal conspirators were apprehended, among whom were two of the sons of Junius Brutus. It was absolutely necessary that some should be made examples of, to deter others from attempting the restoration of Tarquin and destroying the liberty of Rome. To effect this it was that Lucius Junius Brutus, one of the consuls of Rome, in the presence of the Roman people, sat judge and condemned his own sons as traitors to their country. And to give the last proof of his exalted virtue and his love of liberty, he with a firmness of mind only becoming so great a man caused their heads to be struck off in his own presence. When he observed that his rigid virtue occasioned a sort of horror among the people, it is observed that he said only, 'My fellow citizens, do not think that this proceeds from any want of natural affection. No, the death of the sons of Brutus can affect Brutus only. But the loss of liberty will affect my country.'

"Thus highly was liberty esteemed in those days, that a father could sacrifice his sons to save his country. But why do I go to heathen Rome to bring instances of the love of liberty? The best blood in Britain has been shed in the cause of liberty; and the freedom we enjoy at this day may be said to be in a great measure owing to the glorious stand the famous Hampden, and others of our countrymen, made against the arbitrary demands and illegal impositions of the times in which they lived; who, rather than give up the rights of Englishmen and submit to pay an illegal tax of no more, I think, than three shillings, resolved to undergo, and for the liberty of their country did undergo, the greatest extremities in that arbitrary and terrible Court of the Star Chamber, to whose arbitrary proceedings — it being composed of the principal men of the realm, and calculated to support arbitrary government — no bounds or limits could be set, nor could any other hand remove the evil but Parliament."[1]

"Power may justly be compared to a great river. While kept within its due bounds it is both beautiful and useful. But when it overflows its banks, it is then too impetuous to be stemmed; it bears down all before it, and brings destruction and desolation wherever it comes. If, then, this is the nature of power, let us at least do our duty, and like wise men who value freedom use our utmost care to support liberty, the only bulwark against lawless power, which in all ages has sacrificed to its wild lust and boundless ambition the blood of the best men that ever lived.

"I hope to be pardoned, Sir, for my zeal upon this occasion. It is an old and wise caution that when our neighbor's house is on fire we ought to take care of our own. For though — blessed be God — I live in a government where liberty is well understood and freely enjoyed, yet experience has shown us all — I am sure it has to me — that a bad precedent in one government is soon set up for an authority in another. And therefore I cannot but think it my, and every honest man's, that while we pay all due obedience to men in authority we ought at the same time to be upon our guard against power wherever we apprehend that it may affect ourselves or our fellow subjects.

"I am truly very unequal to such an undertaking on many accounts. You see that I labor under the weight of many years, and am bowed down with great infirmities of body. Yet, old and weak as I am, I should think it my duty, if required, to go to the utmost part of the land where my services could be of any use in assisting to quench the flame of prosecutions upon informations, set on foot by the government to deprive a people of the right of remonstrating and complaining, too, of the arbitrary attempts of men in power."

Now Hamilton spoke for the ages in words that were quoted (unfortunately without giving him due credit) 229 years later in the landmark case of *New York Times Company v. Sullivan* when the principles of freedom of the press were extended to include statements — even paid advertisements — that were false, possibly injurious, but not done with intent or malice on the part of the publisher.

"Men who injure and oppress the people under their administration provoke them to cry out and complain, and then make that very complaint the foundation for new oppressions and prosecutions. I wish I could say that there were no instances of this kind.

"But to conclude. The question before the Court and you, Gentlemen of the Jury, is not of small or private concern. It is not the cause of one poor printer, nor of New York alone, which you are now trying. No! It may in its consequence affect every free man that lives under a British government on the main of America. It is the best cause. It is the cause of liberty. And I make no doubt but your upright conduct this day will not only entitle you to the love and esteem of your fellow citizens, but every man who prefers freedom to a life of slavery will bless and honor you as men who have baffled the attempt of tyranny, and by an impartial and uncorrupt verdict have laid a noble foundation for securing to ourselves, our posterity, and our neighbors, that to which nature and the laws of our country have given us a right to liberty of both exposing and opposing arbitrary power (in these parts of the world at least) by speaking and writing truth."

Here Mr. Attorney observed that Mr. Hamilton had gone very much out of the way, and had made himself and the people very merry; but that he had been citing cases not at all to the purpose. All that the jury had to consider was Mr. Zenger's printing and publishing two scandalous libels that very highly reflected on His

Excellency and the principal men concerned in the administration of this government which is confessed. That is, the printing and publishing of the journals set forth in the information is confessed. He concluded that as Mr. Hamilton had confessed the printing, and there could be no doubt but they were scandalous papers highly reflecting upon His Excellency and on the principal magistrates in the Province — therefore he made no doubt but that the jury would find the defendant guilty, and would refer to the Court for their directions.

MR. CHIEF JUSTICE. "Gentlemen of the Jury: The great pains Mr. Hamilton has taken to show how little regard juries are to pay to the opinion of judges, and his insisting so much upon the conduct of some judges in trials of this kind, is done no doubt with a design that you should take but very little notice of what I might say upon this occasion. I shall therefore only observe to you that as the facts or words in the information are confessed, the only thing that can come in question before you is whether the words as set forth in the information make a libel. And that is a matter of law, no doubt, and which you may leave to the Court."

MR. HAMILTON. "I humbly beg Your Honor's pardon, I am very much misapprehended if you suppose that what I said was so designed.

"Sir, you know I made an apology for the freedom that I found myself under a necessity of using upon this occasion. I said there was nothing personal designed. It arose from the nature of our defense."

With that last exchange the judge, once again, tried to undercut Hamilton's argument that the jury was competent only to decide if the words printed by Zenger constituted a libel and that the points of law were for the court, itself, to decide. The twelve men withdrew to make their decision but returned in a remarkably short time. Being asked by the clerk whether they were agreed on their verdict and whether John Peter Zenger was guilty of printing and publishing the libels in the information mentioned, they answered through Thomas Hunt, their foreman: "Not guilty."

Zenger noted that upon announcement of the jury's verdict "there were three huzzas in the hall, which was crowded with people; and the next day I was discharged from my imprisonment." Modestly, he did not offer all the story of his triumph. The reception of the verdict by the crowd was enormous. Reflecting public approval of this rebuff to the unpopular governing elite, shouts of joy filled the hall. The chief justice tried to bring some order to his courtroom, even threatening some of those present with arrest and imprisonment. During this outburst and while the judges were vainly trying to reestablish order in the courtroom, a man, proclaiming himself to be the son of Admiral Sir John Norris,[2] and son-in-law of Lewis Morris, shouted that "applause was common in Westminster Hall and loudest upon the acquittal of the Seven Bishops." Since the man was also one of those most responsible for the cheering, DeLancey felt himself defeated and left the courtroom to the jubilant crowd. The uproar continued culminating in another congratulatory dinner at the Black Horse Tavern. Unfortunately, Zenger was still in custody and not able to enjoy the triumph personally.

As a further gesture of popular approval for the success of both lawyer and client, the city council of New York voted Hamilton "Freedom of the City" for "the remarkable service done by him to the city and colony by his learned and generous defense of the rights of mankind, and the liberty of the Press." This was a distinction he recalled with pride for the remainder of his life — another six years to the exact day. The certificate of freedom was enclosed in a five-and-a-half-ounce gold box described as "splendid," on which were the arms of the city entwined with the following words: *Demensae Sleges — Timefacta Libertas — Haec tandem emergunt.* And in a flying garter were the words: *Non nummis, virtute paratur.* And on the front were the words: *Ita cuique eveniat ut de republica meruit.*[3] The next day, as Hamilton was being taken across the North River to Morrisania on the start of his return to Philadelphia, a grand salute of cannon was fired in his honor.

XII

The Fallout

Establishment of Truth as a Defense

A truly brief account of Zenger's acquittal appeared in the *New York Weekly Journal* in the very first issue for which Zenger was able to get back on the job. By then, however, Zenger's tumultuous vindication had already descended upon the already unpopular Governor Cosby, who found himself increasingly the laughingstock of his "subjects." He took out his revenge by secretly firing Van Dam from the Council (the law suit against Van Dam had fulfilled the popular expectation of its going poorly for the plaintiff). Cosby also took the precaution — on his deathbed the following March — of seeing that Van Dam would not by some accident assume the governorship again. He swore in his loyal supporter George Clarke as his lieutenant. By October 1736, seven months later, Van Dam's numerous friends were on the verge of taking armed action on his behalf when a ship arrived from London with a message that confirmed Cosby's decision.

Cosby's effectiveness in office had been dealt a body blow when the Zenger affair backfired so resoundingly. By now there were "Morrisite" majorities in each legislative body of the combined provinces, and any governor's ability to administer effectively in this atmosphere was gravely hindered. However, his death removed the necessity for his slow-moving superiors to take any action, and with his demise, the current furor lost its focus and soon died down. Cosby was, however, spared the further indignity of seeing Zenger's *Narrative* in print, for it did not appear until three months after his death.

In late March, following the governor's death, William Bradford felt obligated to print a long apology for having misinformed the public about the state of Cosby's health in an earlier issue, but then proceeded to chide Zenger for having maligned the publisher and his *Gazette*.

"But as all men are liable to Mistakes, so more especially the Publisher of a News Paper; for let him be never so careful, he will sometimes have the wrong Intelligence; and therefore we often find in the *English* Papers that they give notice that they had wrong information in such an affair mentioned in such a Paper, and this is allowed of and the Publisher is not charged with *Falsehood*, or a *Publisher of Untruths*. And I hereby acquaint my Friends and Readers, that if at any time I am made sensible that thro' wrong Information I have published anything not true, I shall readily make known the true matter of facts....

"I make this short Apology in my own defence, and not to begin a Controversie or Paper War with *Zenger's Journal*, or its Coadjutors...."

Two years after the trial, and in a further demonstration of popular approval of his actions, Zenger was appointed to the post of official printer to the New York Assembly, and a year later to that of New Jersey. But in those tasks his lack of sophistication (without the supportive reportorial and editorial skills of Alexander) caught up with him. Very soon he lost both positions because — as the appointing committee of the New York Assembly stated — it had found him to be "an indifferent printer and very ignorant of the English language." Given the fluctuating meanings of the word "indifferent," however, one is tempted to question if the legislature was displeased more with the quality of his typesetting or the dispassionateness with which he recorded their proceedings.

The *Pennsylvania Gazette*, Ben Franklin's newspaper, reprinted in its issue of 11 May 1738, a lengthy excerpt from a letter sent to one of its correspondents from London:

We have been lately amused with Zenger's Trial, which has become the *common* Topic of Conversation in all the Coffee Houses, both at the Court-End of Town and in the City. During my Observation, there has not been any piece, published here, so greedily read and so highly applauded. The greatest Men at the Bar have openly declared, that the Subject of Libels was never so well treated at *Westminster-Hall*, as at New York. Our political Writers of different Factions, who never agreed in any thing else, have mentioned the Trial in their public Writings with an Air of Rapture and Triumph. A *Goliath* in Learning and Politics gave his opinion of Mr. *Hamilton's* Argument in these terms, *If it is not Law it is better than Law, it Ought to be Law, and Will Always be Law wherever Justice prevails.* The Tryal has been reprinted four times in three months, and there has been a greater demand for it, by all ranks and degrees of People, than there has been known for any of the most celebrated Performances of our greatest Geniuses. We look upon *Zenger's* Advocate, as *a glorious Assertor of Public Liberty and of the Rights and Privileges of Britons.*

Along with the five editions of Zenger's "Tryal" printed in London alone, it certainly became the most famous publication in America before John Dickinson's *Letters from a Farmer in Pennsylvania* (1767–68).[1] Zenger, however, continued unruffled in the practice of his trade — printing the *Charter of the City of New York* in 1735[2] and the complaint to the provincial assembly that brought about the reinstatement of Alexander and Smith in 1736. During these years, when he was also printer to both the New York and New Jersey assemblies, he taught "the art and mystery of printing" to the son of his first marriage, who entitled himself "John Zenger, Jnr."

After losing the two assembly accounts, Zenger put out numerous items that are still to be found in rare work collections. His *New York Weekly Journal* lasted for several years after his death on 28 July 1746, being carried on first by his widow, Anna, until her death and then, for three more years, by his oldest son.[3] By that time, the media ownership in New York had undergone yet another dramatic change — the James Parker who had run away from his apprenticeship with Bradford in 1733 had reappeared as the assembly's printer and had taken over the *Gazette*, amalgamating it into his *New York Post Boy*, later to become simply the *Post*. Its issue of 4 August 1746 informed the public that "On Monday Evening last, departed this life Mr. John Peter Zenger, in the 49th year of his Age. He has left a Wife and six Children behind; He was a Loving Husband, and a tender Father, and his Death is much lamented by his Family and Relations."[4]

In retrospect Zenger appears to have been a thorough journalist in that if he ran any account he ran it in full. He never attempted to reach the exalted level of intellectualism sought by Keimer, but he was thorough in what he did. The *Journal*, however, had served its purpose by the time of his death, and Parker's *Post Boy* carried the news on 1 July 1751 that Zenger's press and materials were for sale.

Less than a year later, in its issue of 25 May 1752, the *Post Boy* (joined now with the *Gazette*) carried the news of the death of one of its own founders. "Last Saturday Evening departed this life Mr. William Bradford, Printer of this city in the 94th Year of his Age.... He was a true Englishman, and his Complaisance and Affection to his Wives, of which he had two, was peculiarly great; and without the least exaggeration it may be said, that what he had acquired with the first, by the same Carriage was lost with the second...." Printer to the New York government for upwards of fifty years, Bradford was buried in the Trinity churchyard.

Reactions in legal circles to the landmark *Zenger* decision were mixed and initially unsupportive of the new precedent. The foremost example of rejecting the *Zenger* position occurred when the eminent analyst and writer on English law, William Blackstone, published his monumental *Commentaries* (1765–69), in which he upheld the position that freedom of the press meant no more than freedom from the shackles of prior restraint.[5] Once something was printed, the publisher was fair game for anyone who might have been offended by statements thus made public: "Every free man has an undoubted right to lay what sentiments he pleases before the public: to forbid this is to destroy the freedom of the press; but if he publishes what is improper, mischievous, or illegal, he must take the consequences of his own temerity." But Blackstone's was the last gasp of a dying concept.

A more significant sign of the change, as the common law evolved on both sides of the Atlantic, came in 1770 when Alexander McDougall, a leader of the Sons of Liberty, an American revolutionary society, was indicted by a grand jury for libeling the then loyalist-dominated New York Assembly.[6] His supporters simply reprinted Zenger's *Narrative* and the case was quietly and quickly dropped. Zenger's acquittal had registered firmly with all the authorities of New York.

That same year, however, back in England, William Murray (1705–1783) the first earl of Mansfield and a prominent British jurist, heard the case of one Bingley, printer of the weekly newspaper *The North Briton*. Lord Mansfield instructed the jury to determine only if Bingley had, in fact, been the printer. The jury having made that determination, Mansfield dealt with the rest of the libel case as a matter of established law. It is interesting, though, that two years later, in 1772, Mansfield heard another and far more precedential case — that of one Somersett. Though this was a slavery (not a libel) issue, Mansfield's decision harkened forward two centuries to *New York Times Company v. Sullivan* (1964), the current ruling case in American law on libel, which also dealt — at heart — with slavery, or with its residue, in the United States. Somersett had been purchased in Virginia and was being held in chains aboard a ship in the Thames. Several Quakers had brought a suit asking for his freedom since slavery was by then illegal in England. Mansfield ruled that he should be released, stating that this form of bondage was "so odious" that nothing "could be suffered to support it."

In 1776 when the third assembly of the Continental Congress started putting its collective thoughts on paper, its Declaration of Independence was phrased in the name of "the people"; divine right and all that antiquated cant were completely gone. A dozen years later, after its framers had worked in secrecy through the Philadelphia summer, the Preamble to the Constitution of the United States was opened with the ringing words: "We, the people...." Andrew Hamilton had evoked—in the minds of more than those twelve men on the Zenger jury—the concept that ultimate authority for determination of all manner of truth lay with the people who had to live with it. In this, he and Zenger had created an entirely new concept among nations, and one which remains uniquely American even two centuries later. Most other nations, in their legal codes, make it clear that final authority rests with the state; in the British Commonwealth—where most modern concepts of liberty and self-determination started—the operative term is still the "Crown."

In 1792 Parliament passed a law, known to history as "Fox's Libel Act," after its foremost advocate, the British parliamentarian, Charles James Fox,[7] which set into statute the contention advanced unsuccessfully by William Bradford a century earlier and more successfully by Andrew Hamilton, that a jury could return a verdict on both fact and law in libel cases.

In 1812, after the furor over the Federalist-inspired Sedition Acts had pretty much died down, the Supreme Court of the United States ruled there was no criminal common law in the United States; therefore, the legal charge which had been used against Zenger could never rear its ugly head in a federal court. This ruling, however, as shown in the following chapter, had no relevance to cases brought under the libel laws of the various states—such as Alabama.

Finally, in 1843, the Whig politician, Lord John Campbell, towards the end of his long parliamentary career,[8] pushed through an act which stated unequivocally that truth could always be pleaded as a defense for the charge of seditious libel in the courts of Great Britain.

Yet there were setbacks. In Great Britain, then legally united under one parliament with Ireland, the Treason Felony Act was hurriedly passed in April 1848. This law was aimed at suppressing some of the unrest then rampant in Ireland due specifically to the total collapse of the potato crop, but generally to centuries of absentee exploitation. Under the terms of this law, "any person who, by open and advisably speaking, compassed the intimidation of the Crown or Parliament" was punishable by "transportation" for life.

Several persons were tried, found guilty and sentenced under this act. Thomans Francis Meager and William Scott O'Brien were charged with having made seditious speeches and John Mitchell with having published seditious articles in his weekly *United Irishman*. There is little disagreement that these men had advocated a variety of measures that were extremely distasteful to Her Majesty's government — the worst of their offenses being the persistent and correct contention that the English Parliament was in no way representative of the Irish people. Meager and O'Brien were transported to Tasmania and Mitchell to Bermuda.[9]

Under this same act, however, another Irish leader, Charles Gavan Duffy (1816–1903), was tried five times before juries of his "peers," (which included no Catholics, but he managed by his personal eloquence to escape conviction. He was then elected a member of Parliament (1852–55), emigrated voluntarily to Australia, became prime minister of the new dominion and was knighted by Queen Victoria in 1873.

Another significant setback was the failure of the American Constitution to prevent the continuation of "involuntary servitude"— indeed, by its relative silence, in effect to endorse it.[10] Scholars of American history are unanimous in the opinion that for the framers of 1787 to have pressed this issue further in either direction, would have made the Union itself impossible — a judgment confirmed by events three generations after ratification. Thus, the delegates maneuvered around the "peculiar institution," and the best that the protagonists of total human freedom could do was insert a clause limiting importation of slaves after 1808. This institution and its aftermath continued to affect the nation and its liberties. It was in confrontation with the aftermath of human bondage, many years later, that the nation secured, not only the gains of the civil rights movement, but the most recent fruition of news media freedom.

Despite the adoption of the American Bill of Rights, before even a decade had passed, a strongly Federalist Congress enacted the *Sedition Act* of 1798, which imposed up to $5,000 in criminal penalties and five years in prison "if any person shall write, print, utter or publish ... any false, scandalous and malicious writing or writings against the government of the United States, or either house of the Congress ... or the President ... with the intent to defame ... or to bring them, or either of them, into contempt or disrepute; or to excite against them, or either or any of them the hatred of the good people of the United States." One of the few saving graces of this act was its provision that a jury would be the judges of both the law and the facts — exactly as Hamilton had said Zenger's jury ought to be.

Because this act, of greatly questionable constitutionality, expired of its own terms on 3 March 1801, coincident with the end of John Adams' term as president, it was never tested before the largely Federalist Supreme Court, which is probably a very good thing. Most of the justices were Adams appointees, and several had personally expressed themselves in the act's favor. But thoughtful opinion remained on the side of allowing robust political debate, and the act was widely perceived among the people to be "un–American" (though this particular description had yet to come into the nation's lexicon). With the election of Thomas Jefferson in the autumn of 1800 along with a Congress of more liberal bent, there was never a hope of its renewal. All subsequent judicial authorities and scholars have been unanimous in their opinion of the act's impropriety; Thomas Jefferson pardoned those convicted under it, and both he and various courts remitted the fines that had been levied for convictions. Parenthetically, it should be noted that throughout Unites States' history, courts have generally shown themselves to be more restrictive of personal liberties, when taken to excess, than have commentators on the law in general.

However, an interesting turn of events took place in court in 1803 — like the *Zenger* case in New York and also argued on behalf of a free press by a lawyer named Hamilton. One Croswell, publisher of the *Hudson Balance* was charged by the state's attorney general, Ambrose Spencer, with criminal libel in a convoluted matter having political implications equal to those of Zenger's prosecution. The case came before New York's Chief Justice Lewis, who held that in a criminal trial for libel the truth could not be admitted in evidence and that the jury was merely to decide the fact of publication, the question of libel being for the court to decide — the very same set of circumstances and positions that had been demolished by Andrew Hamilton eighty years earlier. Upon appeal to the entire bench, the attorney general rehearsed the arguments used by Bradley in defending the judgement handed down by Lewis. Alexander Hamilton — the same whose portrait adorns the American ten dollar bill — appearing, as did his predecessor, as a volunteer on behalf of a free press, denounced the ancient maxim attributed to Sir Matthew Hale[11] that "the greater the truth, the greater the libel" as being wholly inconsistent with American ideals. The court, after long deliberation found itself deadlocked in a tie, and so Justice Lewis's holding stood.

This case brought on such an uproar within the state of New York that a few years later — in Chapter 130 of its general laws — the legislature voted the following: "No reporter, editor, or proprietor of any newspaper shall be liable to any action, civil or criminal, for a fair and true report in such newspaper of any judicial, legislative, or other public official proceedings of any statement, speech, argument, or debate in the course of same, except upon actual proof of malice." A further provision restricted this protection to the actual reportage itself, so that it did not extend to editorial commentary.

Another setback case came in 1825 when an action was brought before the United States court for the district of Missouri. Judge James Hawkins Peck decided a Spanish land grant issue against the heirs of Antoine Soulard, and they appealed his decision. Judge Peck then published an elaborate defense of his opinion in the *Missouri Republican*, which was followed a few days later by a reply in the *Inquirer*, written by the attorney for the heirs. Judge Peck considered this act as one of contempt of his court and caused the editor to be arrested. He followed this up by sentencing the lawyer to twenty-four hours in prison and eighteen months' suspension from the bar. As a result of this, Judge Peck himself was impeached in May 1830 and tried before the United States Senate. Judge Peck was sustained in his office by the margin of twenty-two to twenty-one after an impassioned plea by William Wirt of Virginia,[12] who gave the best possible argument in favor of restraint of press freedom:

> It is said that in punishing this publication as a contempt the judge has invaded the liberty of the Press. What is the liberty of the Press, and in what does it consist? Does it consist in a right to vilify the tribunals of the country, and to bring them into contempt by gross and wanton misrepresentations of their proceedings? Does it consist in a right to obstruct and corrupt the streams of justice by poisoning the public mind with regard to causes in these tribunals before they are heard? Is this a correct idea of the liberty of the Press? If so, the defamer has a charter as free as the winds, provided he resort to the Press for the propagation of his slander, and, under the prostituted sanction of the liberty of the Press, hoary age and virgin innocence lie at his mercy. This is not the idea of liberty of the Press which prevails in courts of justice, or which exists in any sober or well-regulated mind. The liberty of the Press is among the greatest of blessings, civil and political, so long as it is directed to its proper object — that of disseminating correct and useful information among the people. But this greatest of blessings may become

the greatest of curses if it shall be permitted to burst its proper barriers. The liberty of the Press has always been the favorite watchword of those who live by its licentiousness. It has been from time immemorial, is still, and ever will be the perpetual decantatum of all libelers. ... To be useful, the liberty of the Press must be restrained. The principle of restraint was imposed upon every part of creation. By restraint the planets were kept in their orbits. The earth performed its regular evolutions by the restraint of the centrifugal force operating upon it. The vine would shoot into rank luxuriance if not under the restraint of the laws of nature, by which every thing was preserved within its proper bounds. Was not every thing on earth impressed with this principle? And was not the liberty of the Press to be restrained to the performance of its rightful functions of propagating truth for just ends?

This was Wirt's last hurrah; he died the following year. As an attorney, he had been defense counsel for journalist James Thomson Callender, who had been charged under the Alien and Sedition Acts. Callender, another journalist who cared — and dared — to print the unwelcome truth, was not convicted, but died soon afterwards (by drowning while intoxicated). There was a sequel to the Peck case: though exonerating the judge, Congress soon passed a law that clarified (and restricted) the conditions under which federal courts were allowed to punish for contempt.

The acquittal of Judge Peck by the United States Senate gave heart to many others who would restrain freedom of accurate expression. Among the victims of this courage was Donn Piatt, grandson of one of George Washington's staff officers and a vigorously outspoken nonbeliever in Negro slavery.[13] Piatt, the descendant of Huguenots, was a lawyer and jurist of Ohio. Migrating to the national arena, he became secretary and chargé d'affaires of the American legation in Paris and then a strong supporter of Abraham Lincoln. After service in the Civil War, in 1874, his sixty-fifth year, he founded a weekly newspaper in the nation's capital, appropriately entitled the *Washington Capital*. Endowed with a quick and penetrating wit, he used his medium of expression to great and pointed effect: "The Democratic party represents [that of] organized ignorance; the Republican party, that of organized greed...." Elsewhere, he wrote that "[t]he United States Senate is the Cave of the Winds...." For an ongoing series of this kind of perceptive but unwelcome comment, he was indicted two years later for "inciting rebellion, insurrection and riot." But as one biographer noted: "though he tried very hard, he never got into jail." Piatt, a worrisome gadfly to the political elite, also coined the apt description of what was then a cornerstone of American foreign policy: "twisting the British lion's tail." Able to remain at large, he sold his newspaper for a substantial profit and retired to the more tranquil environment of his southwest Ohio birthplace, where he took a seat in the state legislature.

XIII
Subsequent Events
Zenger's Subsequent Example

One intriguing sidebar to the evolution of the concept of journalistic freedom came in Bavaria, the original homeland of John Peter Zenger. During the Austro-Prussian (Seven Weeks) War of 1866 — one of the several quasi–comic opera conflicts by which the kingdom of Prussia asserted its right to unify the various independent states of Germany — the Bavarian army, fighting on the Austrian side, performed with less glory than many people of that proud state had expected. Afterwards, an article making this point appeared in the Munich *Volksbote für den Bürger und Landmann* under a date of 19 October 1866. After this article had been read and, presumably, snickered at, the chief of the Bavarian General Staff brought suit against the editor, Ernst Zander (1803–1872), claiming a libelous defamation. However, when the case reached the jury three months later, the editor was triumphantly vindicated, amid great popular applause since the verdict was perceived as a public condemnation of the manner in which the Bavarian army had been led.[1]

Ludwig Samson Arthur von der Tann, the fifty-one-year-old target of these editorial ministrations, was the victim of a lot of political indecision. His commander-in-chief, Prince Charles, was a member of the Bavarian royal family and responded to the politics of the numerous minor German states that formed a loose alliance to counter the growing power of the expansionist Hohenzollern rulers of Prussia. When the politicians, gathered at Frankfurt, demanded — and got — military protection, the separate armies of the smaller states never merged with that of Austria. As a result of their not hanging together, the Prussians were able to hang them all separately. Since members of the royal family were then above that sort of blame, it was von der Tann who, rather unfairly, took the heat.

There was another major development that impacted on American history, but with a more peripheral relationship to freedom of speech. In their day of greatest need, the American colonies received significant help from the absolutist government of King Louis XVI of France. This was not given out of love for a bunch of revolutionaries — after all, Louis and his Austrian wife were themselves soon to fall victim to some of that ilk among their own subjects. But French ambitions had been badly abused by the British in recent years, most particularly with respect to their North American possessions and activities. Thus, lending assistance to this newest thorn in the side of George III was less an act of charity for these irreverent, downtrodden colonials than another tit-for-tat move in the long-playing contest between two traditional European enemies.

The American representatives in France took pains not to invoke any theories of democratic government in seeking assistance; they were only interested in getting whatever help they could. The persuasiveness of Benjamin Franklin (who taught himself French at age seventy, just for this mission), John Adams and John Jay[2] ultimately carried the day with Lafayette and his genre, but they obviously did not rely on sales pitches based on concepts of human freedom and abstract theories of popular government. That would surely have been a tough sell in the court of Louis XVI. (Some of the concepts developed in Jefferson's *Declaration* of course soon did find their way across the ocean, through the language barrier into French liberal thinking.) However derived, French help was crucial, particularly in its timing, for the fortuitous presence of a strong fleet under Admiral François De Grasse (1722–1788) was what forced the surrender of Cornwallis at Yorktown and brought the British to the peace table. The fact that De Grasse had the courage — or foolhardiness — to bring his fleet close to the coast during hurricane season, thus outmaneuvering the more cautious Thomas Graves of the English navy, is a little appreciated sidelight of American history. But the ties of heredity, language, legal tradition, literature, commerce (most immediately) and family survived the War for Independence and brought the English and American peoples back together, despite the acrimony of even a second war in 1812.

It has also been argued that the adoption by the French National Assembly of the *Declaration of the Rights of Man and of the Citizen* aided in the adoption of the *American Bill of Rights*. Much of the language is quite similar, and the French action took place only a few weeks before the congressional vote on the first ten amendments. A copy of the French opus could easily have made it to American soil on a fast ship. Did the

Congress have the benefit of Abbé Sieyès's work? The American Bill of Rights was already well-advanced by then, so this question needed not be answered. In any case, the fraternal bonds between the two revolutions soon became irrelevant in practice when the French Revolution got out of hand, French ships began attacking American vessels and the famous XYZ Affair scandalized the U.S.

The concept of individual, human rights found its most fertile soil in the United States. Three generations after the nation's founding, with the issue of slavery on everyone's mind, the American Civil War was started over the ostensible and perfectly valid issue of states' rights. Could a state that had voluntarily entered the Union decide of itself to withdraw? But, in taking up the fight, the Union was motivated not only by the Mrs. Howe's "Battle Hymn of the Republic," but by the value of human rights — the right of *all* the people to decide for themselves what was good for them and what was right and true — the same concept which had been so brilliantly verbalized by Andrew Hamilton in defending that "indifferent printer" John Peter Zenger.

From the ratification of the Constitution, that concept had dwelt in all portions of the United States, but appeared in varying intensities and with different expressions. Despite the ringing and long-lasting rhetoric of the Virginian Thomas Jefferson, the North was basically more liberal with respect to the specific issue of slavery, for its elimination had little economic impact in that area. Massachusetts, for instance, had outlawed slavery even before there was a Constitution and a Union; abolitionists could thrive freely in its political and economic atmosphere.[3] And while many spoke vigorously against the "peculiar institution," those who did so were also largely unwilling to recognize that slaves were a major asset of "property" in the economy of their "owners." As far back as the Magna Carta, the promise was on record not to take anyone's property without prompt compensation. But compensation to slaveowners was never seriously discussed prior to 1860, and in the bitter aftermath of the Civil War that idea was completely forgotten.

Within the infant Union in the South there were differences, too. The slave-to-master ratio differed greatly among those states (see Table 1). That ratio could be used to explain why North Carolina, for instance, has always been regarded (in the North, anyway) as the most liberal of the original southern states, and South Carolina as the most reactionary — South Carolina had more than twice as many slaves per free citizen as North Carolina. When the new nation first took a careful head count, in 1790, the official numbers came out as shown in Table 1.

Table 1: Results of the 1790 Census

STATE	FREE	SLAVE	SLAVES PER THOUSAND FREEMEN*	TOTAL POP.
N.H.	141,727	158	1	141,885
Mass.	378,787	0	0	378,787
R.I.	67,877	948	14	68,825
Conn.	235,182	2,764	12	237,946
N.Y.	318,796	21,324	67	340,120
N.J.	172,716	11,423	66	184,139
Penn.	430,636	3,737	9	434,373
Del.	50,209	8,887	177	59,096
Md.	216,692	103,036	475	319,728
Va.	454,983	292,627	643	747,610
N.C.	293,179	100,572	343	393,751
S.C.	141,979	107,094	754	249,073
Ga.	53,284	29,264	549	82,548
TOTAL	2,956,047	681,834	231	3,637,881[4]

*Rounded to the nearest whole number.

The evolution of human freedoms in America as well as elsewhere, therefore, varied regionally to a large degree. In the North, while there linger some apocryphal stories that after 1850 "No Irish Need Apply," controversy over civil or human rights was basically nonexistent. Claims of such discrimination against the Irish are belied by the eminence achieved by a number of pre–Revolutionary figures of Irish ancestry. New Hampshire's leader in Revolutionary fighting was General John Sullivan, whose massive prestige ultimately ensured that state's acceptance of the 1787 constitution; and the governor of Massachusetts during the locally unpopular War of 1812 was James Sullivan, who (inter alia) appointed Samuel Putnam, this author's great, great, great grandfather, a man of unanimously English/Puritan ancestry, to be Chief Justice of the Commonwealth's Supreme Judicial Court. The difference relative to the Irish who emigrated from their homeland in the mid-nineteenth century may be in the fact that the earlier emigrants brought education and property with them, whereas the latter, being the victims of centuries of English economic and cultural persecution, had nothing to bring and were welcomed accordingly.

While in the North blacks may have been held to second-class status as respects their acceptance into society or their participation in the economy, the law was not explicitly against them. Massachusetts' and the nation's first hero of the revolutionary conflict, after all, was Crispus Attucks, a freed black slave who was one of the five killed by the British in the Boston "Massacre"; to most people the other four individuals remain honorably anonymous. Thus, in the North, the state laws of libel were never used to suppress the abolitionist press, which thrived. Horror stories about slavery, sometimes embellished even beyond reality, abounded, and popular feelings ran high against the return of Dred Scott to bondage.

In legal cases brought under the various state libel laws up until the time of the Civil War, the various state courts each followed their own standards and precedents. The Civil War, however, and its immediate political aftermath changed all that quite dramatically.[5] The Thirteenth Amendment eliminated slavery, and the Fourteenth Amendment applied the conditions of the First Amendment to the individual states, in one giant step making the great majority of libel actions potentially a matter of federal jurisdiction. Thus a plethora of judicial decisions in the various states, particularly those involving any issue of freedom of expression, were suddenly superseded by a new venue: the federal court system of the United States.

For almost a century after the end of the conflict between states' rights and human rights, there was no firm and definitive position taken by the Supreme Court, and libel decisions continued to be tried under a variety of localized precedents. But that all changed in the landmark case of *New York Times Company v. Sullivan* (1964), where the issue of truth in libel was moved slightly to one side and the issue of "malice" became critical. Thus, while the trial of Zenger in 1735 was settled by popular approval of his version of truth, the definitive precedent today requires the court to ask this question: "Did the publisher know the truth before he printed the non-truth?" If he did, and *recklessly* expressed a significant non-truth, then there exists evidence of "malice." Whether or not the statement was that of the publisher — i.e., editorial content — or that of an advertiser made no difference to the *New York Times* court. The non-lawyer should note that in this context the word "malice" does not imply an intent to do evil or wrong, but rather the intentional lack of desire to be aware of the truth.

In the lawyer's "bible," *Prosser on Torts,*[6] the chapter on *Constitutional Privilege* begins with the following paragraphs, which we might review by way of background for Chapter XV's discussion of *New York Times Company v. Sullivan,* the final word on freedom of expression in the United States of America.

Prior to 1964 there had been occasional mention in the cases dealing with both defamation and privacy, of the guarantee of freedom of speech and of the press contained in the First Amendment to the Constitution of the United States. It was usually mentioned as an argument in support of a decision at common law holding that the particular conduct of the defendant was privileged. In 1964, in the famous case of the *New York Times Co. v. Sullivan*, the Supreme Court of the United States introduced something of a bombshell by holding that the First Amendment itself required the privilege. A series of subsequent decisions, in both the federal and the state courts, have resulted in taking over under the aegis of the Constitution a large area of privileges, and in the process considerably broadening them beyond the scope within which they had previously been recognized. This is unquestionably the greatest victory won by defendants in the modern history of the law of torts.

The background of the *Sullivan* case lay in the general recognition, at common law, of a qualified privilege in defamation actions, of what was called "fair comment" upon the conduct and qualifications of public officers and public employees. Unlike the privilege of complaint to officials, this broader privilege extended to publication to the public in general of a matter of public concern.

While the existence of this privilege was undisputed, there was disagreement as to whether it was restricted to statements expressing only "comment" or opinion, as distinct from misstatements of fact. Some three-fourths of the state courts which considered the question held that the privilege of public discussion was limited to opinion, criticism and comment, and did not extend to any false assertion of fact. The reason usually given was, that while men in public life must expect to be subjected to public comment, opinion and criticism, they were not to be made the victims of misrepresentation as to the facts without redress, lest desirable candidates be deterred from seeking office, and the public interest suffer.

There was a substantial, and vigorous, minority view that even false statements of fact were privileged, if they were made for the public benefit with an honest belief in their truth, because the public interest demanded that those who are in a position to furnish information about public servants be not deterred by fear of suit, with the resulting necessity of proving the truth of what they say in court. The "opinion" limitation proved to be a most unsatisfactory and unreliable one, difficult to draw in practice: and there is nothing in the history of the minority states to indicate that the rule in any way deterred candidates from seeking office.

XIV
Frank Herbert Simonds
(1878–1936)
A Visionary Journalist in the Zenger Mold

> Frank Herbert Simonds, student of world thought and the mul-
> tiform motives of various peoples; painstaking seeker of knowl-
> edge of national tendencies; lucid in expression, which gift you use
> to interpret complex problems to an eager people; independent in
> judgement and action; quick and accurate in conclusions and
> definite in statement; I confer upon you the honorary degree of
> Doctor of Letters.[1]

It was Cassandra, daughter of Priam the last king of Troy, to whom
Apollo promised the gift of prophecy if she would become his paramour.
The lady accepted his proposal and received the gift, but then changed
her mind — life with Agamemnon appeared more promising. Apollo,
more than slightly put out, thereupon ordained that her predictions
would never be taken seriously.

Prophetically, in the same year that the Austrian engineer Ferdi-
nand Mannlicher invented the repeating rifle, Frank Simonds was born
in Concord, Massachusetts, on 5 April 1878, the only child of William
Henry and Jennie (Garty) Simonds. Jennie died soon after, and some
years later Frank's father, a conductor for the Boston and Maine Rail-
road, remarried. Frank was brought up with two younger stepsisters and
attended Concord High School. Enrolling at Harvard with the class of
1900, and taking time out to serve in the Spanish-American War as a
private, he nonetheless managed to graduate with his class. In subsequent years Frank was proud to tell listeners that his thirty-nine-year-
old great-great-grandfather, Joshua Simonds, Jr., had fought the British
at Lexington.[2] Joshua was not the only Simonds ancestor in the action
at the start of the American Revolution. Before the events of 19 April

1775 were finished, several other of Frank Simonds's ancestors — Nathan Tufts of Medford, Joseph Mason of Lincoln, Isaac Pierce of Waltham as well as Joshua's father-in-law, William Bowers of Billerica — had all taken part.

An avid student of military affairs, young Frank studied the strategic campaigns of Napoleon in detail and, with sets of toy soldiers, had reenacted the tactical decisions of the emperor's battles on the floor of his bedroom. In subsequent years, whenever time permitted, he visited the scenes of military conflict, walking the terrain and memorizing important topographic details.[3] In 1901 he became employed by the *New York Tribune,* and by Christmas of the following year he felt confident enough of his future to marry Mary France Gledhill, a social worker from Albany, by whom he would have two children.[4]

The *Tribune* sent him to Washington as a correspondent in 1903 and to Albany a year later. In 1906 he went to work for the competition, the still celebrated *New York Sun.*[5] In 1908 he became one of its editorial writers and in 1913 he was appointed editor of the Danas' *Evening Sun.* Two years later, in 1915, he returned to the *Tribune* as associate editor and was assigned to cover the conflict raging in Europe. This was the task for which he had unwittingly prepared in his childhood. The knowledge gained from his earlier hobby soon became the envy of all his journalistic associates trying to understand what was going on in the global turmoil.

The best of journalists are not those who carry a torch for some cause and see every action as justification for some viewpoint. Instead, the best of journalists are those who constantly strive to see current events in their historic perspective and who prepare themselves for reporting by a thorough background in history. Frank Simonds was the archetype of the best in American journalism.

While the war was still raging in eastern France, at sea, in Poland, the Balkans and Near East, Simonds wrote with particular thoroughness on the enormous bloodletting that occurred in the almost year-long battle for control of the fortress complex at Verdun. For the title of this volume, he used the famous words of General Pétain,[6] the French commander during much of this grueling siege: *They Shall Not Pass — Verdun.* Before the war was over and with the major aspects of his literary career still ahead of him, Dartmouth saw fit to honor Simond's work with the doctoral citation given at the opening of this portrait. And with most others still trying to untangle the conflicting postwar analyses of the global conflict, Simonds published in 1919 his monumental five-volume series entitled *A History of the World War.*

The conflict over, Simonds stayed on to cover the gropings towards peace that began with the Paris Conference of 1919. Assigning himself primarily to cover the League of Nations in Geneva, he attended the almost immediately inconsequential, but at the time well-noted, Locarno Conference and Pact of 1925, where Benito Mussolini successfully bamboozled his European colleagues. He reported on the London Naval Conference of 1930 and, between more immediate tasks, wrote a number of incisive articles on political affairs and their portent.

Soon after the end of World War I, Simonds dropped his exclusive employment with the *Tribune* in order to syndicate his articles dealing with contemporary world affairs. As a spin-off of this endeavor, he compiled the essential elements of his daily observations into a series of volumes, the mere titles of which tell the sad story of ineffective and narrow-minded leadership among the victorious Allies. In their defense, it may be observed that the victorious powers had suffered such an enormous loss of their finest manhood and national treasure at the hands of the aggressive Central Powers that the inability of Allied leadership to hold onto a forward-looking peace policy was understandable. They, even though elected to lead their peoples into "a world safe for democracy," were human enough to want revenge first. As the whole world came to learn, in seeking this retribution, these leaders sowed the seeds for the far worse conflict that overtook the same nations twenty years later. An often overlooked factor in this process was the political humiliation of Germany, which was nevertheless left as one of the world's greatest economic powers.

The titles of Simonds's other books, from 1919 through 1933, can be read as a prophetic litany — *How Europe Made Peace Without America* (1927); *They Won the War* (1931); *Can Europe Keep the Peace?* (1931); *Can America Stay at Home?* (1932); *The ABC of War Debts* (1933); *America Faces the Next War* (1933). In his preface to the last of these books, Simonds refers to the third and fourth of these titles with the following words: "In these works I have discussed the problem of peace or war in Europe and the relation of the United States to that problem. The events of the current year [Hitler's election as chancellor in Germany and the Japanese flouting of the World Court by invasion of Manchuria] produced a situation clearly foreshadowed in those books."

Winning decorations in the immediate postwar years from the governments of France, Belgium, Rumania, Hungary, Poland and Greece,[7] Simonds had also received the first Pulitzer Prize given for the best editorial of the year, which ran in the *New York Tribune* on 7 May 1916.

W. David Sloan has recently summarized the Pulitzer committee's reasons for choosing Simonds's editorial:

> Until the sinking of the ship *Lusitania* on May 7, 1915, Americans were widely split and many were truly neutral toward the contestants in World War I. But a turning point in public opinion came with the sinking.[8] This was the opinion of many historians, including Frank Simonds, editor of the *New York Tribune*. In a multi-volume history of World War I published in 1919, Simonds says that with the sinking, Americans began to see the true inhumane nature of Germany. Yet at the time of the *Lusitania* tragedy, fewer than half a dozen American papers asked for war. One of those that did was Simonds's *Tribune*. In a show of militant patriotism, it warned that "the nation which remembered the sailors of the *Maine* will not forget the civilians of the *Lusitania*." On the first anniversary of the sinking, Simonds wrote the editorial that won the first Pulitzer Prize. It is an attempt to characterize the European war as one between civilization and barbarism. Though today it may appear extremely simplistic, it did mirror Simonds's true opinion and was not an artificial attempt to appeal to his readers' baser natures. In 1916 the editorial, despite its simplicity, was effective considering the frame of mind of Americans.[9]

As noted by Sloan, the state of mind of the American people at the outbreak of World War I was largely favorable to neutrality. The ancestors of most Americans had bequeathed a legacy to their descendants of deliberate forgetfulness for the concerns of people in those parts of the world they had left behind; wide oceans now separated them from ancient grudges. This attitude had been enunciated by George Washington in his often quoted Farewell Address and ratified twenty years later by the famous Monroe Doctrine. Internally, this state of mind was a powerful and long-lasting force in all parts of the nation except the Northeast and a few centers on the West Coast. So powerful was the sentiment of isolationism in the face of the obviously changing world conditions of communication and transportation that it dominated American policy throughout the 1920s and into the 1930s. Isolationism only waned with the beginning of World War II, when the political wisdom and courage of Arthur Vandenberg led the Republican minority in the Senate to a bipartisan foreign policy.[10]

At the outset of World War I, however, Americans who considered themselves of German ancestry were the second largest ethnic group in the country. Their ominous silence in the face of pro–Allied spokesmen of British descent left a wide uncertainty about where this nation might end up as the European conflict ground painfully on. It was thus a major and long-term effort to inform public opinion sufficiently so that American politicians would actually vote to move the nation into a formal conflict with Germany.[11] Despite the eloquence of Simonds's prize-winning editorial, and that of a few other courageous editors,[12] Woodrow Wilson ran for a second term as president in 1916 on the slogan "He Kept Us Out of War."

The preface to Simonds's final book, *The Great Powers in World Politics*[13] was in many ways his most farsighted:

> This book constitutes an attempt to examine the causes and circumstances of this transition from the political chaos of the immediate postwar years to the economic catastrophe which has accompanied the Great Depression. It undertakes to prove that precisely as European peace was impermanent a century ago because of the political inequalities existing in the condition of the nationalities of the Continent, so, today world peace is precarious because of the economic disparities in the circumstances of nations everywhere.
>
> The argument of this volume is that Fascism and National Socialism, although on the surface indistinguishable from familiar nineteenth century imperialism, are at bottom, at least in their latest stages, the characteristic expressions of great peoples in revolt against the limitations placed upon their national prosperity by their poverty in natural resources. The aim of the authors is not to prove that new wars have already become inevitable but simply to demonstrate that no viable system of organized peace can be founded upon the contemporary status quo of economic inequality.
>
> The purpose of this book is to make clear how real and great are the disparities between material resources of the several Great Powers, how disastrous are the consequences of these disparities for the material and social conditions of the people of the less favored countries, and, finally, how idle is the hope that the world can escape new wars so long as no peaceful means can be discovered to abolish inequalities which in the eyes of those who suffer from them seem proof positive of intolerable injustice....

Despite his specialization in foreign affairs, or perhaps because of the esoteric, detached nature of this field, Frank Simonds maintained a close touch with the bare essentials of life. He acquired a multi-acre farm with its house and barns on a north-facing New Hampshire hillside, near where Simonds directed that he was to be buried.[14] He had acquired a substantial acreage on the high ground near the Maine border, mostly from members of the extended Stewart family. Interestingly, given Simonds's antipathy to things British, his farm, in that section of Eaton township known as Snowville, was christened "Blighty" after the British soldiers' wartime term for their homeland.[15] It was at Blighty, with its magnificent view recalling America's first five presidents, that he composed most of the books mentioned in this portrait.

Simonds's most incisive views on the world situation were given during the final year of his life in the form of six Albert Shaw lectures on Diplomatic History at Johns Hopkins University.[16] In these lectures, Simonds noted that at the end of the nineteenth century, the United States was still an "undeveloped" debtor nation to the tune of two billion dollars. By the start of World War I, this foreign debt had risen to some three billion. However, by 1921, even *excluding* the twelve billion in war debts piled up by the Allied belligerents, the balance of payments had so shifted that the world owed the United States more than four billion dollars, a dramatic and disruptive reversal of the global balance sheet.

In postwar years, the American insistence on collecting these debts from the nations of Europe, whose economies were in a shambles anyway, gave this nation the justifiable sobriquet of "Uncle Shylock." Furthermore, only one country, economically tiny Finland, ever set out to adhere to the schedule of repayments demanded. In the meantime, the American trade surplus continued to pile up at the rate of half a billion pre–1929 dollars per year. The emerging global economy could never hope to stand such a one-sided arrangement.

Simonds pointed out further seeds for bitterness. While the Central Powers[17] were militarily defeated — a point few knowledgeable persons ever contested — all parties had agreed to an "armistice" effective on the eleventh hour of the eleventh day of the eleventh month. It was only after the military forces of the Central Powers, notably Germany, had laid down their arms that the people found their leaders had deceived them as to what that "armistice" meant in reality. Beyond that matter, the League of Nations and the World Court both worked in French and were basically managed for the benefit of France. America had isolated itself from the League, and even Britain had reserved the right to decide when and to what extent she would assume any responsibility for enforcing the international body's decisions. But Wilson's famous Fourteen Points (including the widely touted principle of self-determination) had been promised to the defeated nations as the bases of all devolving peace accords. Thus, for example, when Germany and

Austria set out to form a customs union in 1930, France and Italy took the matter to the French–dominated World Court, and the union was denied as contrary to the Versailles Treaty. No consideration at all was given to the freely expressed desires or best interests of the Teutonic nations.

Meantime, on the other side of the world, the Chinese government protested to the World Court about the Japanese invasion of Chinese Manchuria in 1931. In this case, not only had the Japanese voluntarily agreed to various nonaggression arrangements with the Chinese, but they justified their contrary military action on the sole grounds that it was in their own national economic interest. Though in this instance the World Court found in favor of the underdog Chinese, enforcement was another matter. None of the powers that had the ability to enforce the World Court's decisions felt their own interests were sufficiently at stake to stir them to action, and so Manchuria became the Japanese province of Manchukuo until 1945. Nevertheless, Japan quit the League of Nations over the decision.

Simonds pointed out further that in Germany's case when "after fifteen years of vain effort to obtain a revision of the military clauses of the Treaty of Versailles, [the country] finally quit both the Disarmament Conference and the League and presently announced their purpose to rearm in defiance of treaty law, appeal was made again to Geneva. Once more, too, no fair-minded person could fail to perceive the injustice of a law which compelled the great German nation to remain disarmed on an armed continent.... This decision of the council was rendered at the dictation of the French, British, Italian and Soviet representatives, that is, of statesmen whose views were determined not by any concern for the justice of Germany's claims but purely and simply by the fact that justice for Germany might involve insecurity for their own countries. Thus as the Court had been exploited in 1931, the League was employed in 1935 to sustain treaty law which was inconsistent with justice and had been imposed upon defeated peoples by the bayonets of their con-querors."

Blessedly for the people of the world, after the conclusion of the Second World War, the onset of which Simonds had predicted for a dozen years before his death, the fate of the defeated peoples was in the hands of a greatly different style of person than had written the oppressive terms of Versailles. Taking their example from the internationally minded Franklin Roosevelt, Harry Truman and George Catlett Marshall showed the world that they, at least, had learned something from the lessons of history.

Journalists, while endemically suspicious and occupationally trained to be cynical, also tend to recognize merit in their competitors — especially after death. Simonds was particularly honored in this regard by his crosstown competition, the *New York Times,* which carried an editorial on 24 January 1936, the same day as his obituary[18]:

> As an editorial writer on the *Sun* he was especially interested in foreign affairs. Later his studies broadened into the whole field of world politics. His knowledge of them was comprehensive and thorough. He could have rattled off at the typewriter all the European treaties, from that of Verdun[19] eleven hundred years ago, to the latest product of the chancelleries. He was the friend or acquaintance of European statesmen. His works received respectful attention abroad. It was his custom to go over every year to freshen or readjust his impressions. If his judgements seemed sometimes too positive, his conclusions were founded on intimate acquaintance with the subject.
>
> An acknowledged expert in his province, he provoked thought because he was a thinker, and disagreeing critics admired the fullness of his acquirements even if they disputed this and that dictum. He goes in the plenitude of his powers and after a life of manly endeavor....

XV
Final Fruition
Evolution of American
Freedom of the Press

On Tuesday, 29 March 1960, 226 years and 130 days after John Peter Zenger had spent his first night in the jail for inability to raise bail, a full-page advertisement, no "lampoon or pasquinade," appeared in another New York newspaper, the *New York Times*. Entitled *Heed Their Rising Voices*, this piece quoted part of a *Times* editorial that had appeared ten days earlier and then continued:

> As the whole world knows by now, thousands of southern Negro students are engaged in widespread non-violent demonstrations in positive affirmation of the right to live in human dignity as guaranteed by the U.S. Constitution and the Bill of Rights. In their efforts to uphold these guarantees, they are being met by an unprecedented wave of terror by those who would deny and negate that document which the whole world looks upon as setting the pattern for modern freedom....
>
> In Orangeburg, South Carolina, when 400 students peacefully sought to buy their doughnuts and coffee at lunch counters in the business district, they were forcibly ejected, tear-gassed, soaked to the skin in freezing weather with fire hoses, arrested en masse and herded into an open barbed-wire stockade to stand for hours in the bitter cold.
>
> In Montgomery, Alabama, after students sang "My Country 'Tis of Thee" on the State Capitol steps, their leaders were expelled from school, and truckloads of police armed with shotguns and tear-gas ringed the Alabama State College campus. When the entire student body protested to state authorities by refusing to re-register, their dining hall was padlocked in an attempt to starve them into submission.

In Tallahassee, Atlanta, Nashville, Savannah, Greensboro, Memphis, Richmond, Charlotte, and a host of other cities in the South, young American teenagers, in the face of the entire weight of official state apparatus and police power, have boldly stepped forth as protagonists of democracy. Their courage and amazing restraint have inspired millions and given a new dignity to the cause of freedom.

Small wonder that the Southern violators of the Constitution fear this new, non-violent brand of freedom fighter ... even as they fear the upswelling right-to-vote movement. Small wonder that they are determined to destroy the one man who, more than any other, symbolizes the new spirit now sweeping the South — the Rev. Dr. Martin Luther King, Jr., world-famous leader of the Montgomery Bus Protest. For it is his doctrine of non-violence which has inspired and guided the students in their widening wave of sit-ins; and it is this same Dr. King who founded and is president of the Southern Christian Leadership Conference — the organization which is spearheading the surging right-to-vote movement. Under Dr. King's direction the Leadership Conference conducts Student Workshops and Seminars in the philosophy and technique of non-violent resistance.

Again and again the Southern violators have answered Dr. King's peaceful protests with intimidation and violence. They have bombed his home almost killing his wife and child. They have assaulted his person. They have arrested him seven times — for "speeding," "loitering" and similar "offenses." And now they have charged him with "perjury" — a *felony* under which they could imprison him for *ten years*. Obviously, their real purpose is to remove him physically as the leader to whom students and millions of others — look for guidance and support, and thereby intimidate *all* leaders who may rise in the South. Their strategy is to behead this movement, and thus to demoralize Negro Americans and weaken their will to struggle. The defense of Martin Luther King, spiritual leader of the student sit-in movement, clearly, therefore, is an integral part of the total struggle for freedom in the South.

Decent-minded Americans cannot help but applaud the creative daring of the students and the quiet heroism of Dr. King. But this is one of those moments in the stormy history of Freedom when men and women of good will must do more than applaud the rising-to-glory of others. The America whose good name hangs in the balance before a watchful world, the America whose heritage of Liberty these Southern Upholders of the Constitution are defending, is our America as well as theirs....

We must heed their rising voices — yes — but we must add our own.

We must extend ourselves above and beyond moral support and render the material help so urgently needed by those who are taking the risks, facing jail, and even death in a glorious re-affirmation of our Constitution and its Bill of Rights.

We urge you to join hands with our fellow Americans in the South by supporting, with your dollars, this Combined Appeal for all three needs — the defense of Martin Luther King — the support of the embattled students — and the struggle for the right-to-vote.

This full-page advertisement cost some $4,800. Below its main text appeared sixty-six names of prominent Americans, ranging from Harry Belafonte to Eleanor Roosevelt. There followed an additional list of twenty Southern clergymen, who further endorsed the appeal. At the bottom corner appeared a coupon which those interested could cut out and mail in with their contributions and a further list of the members of the "Committee to Defend Martin Luther King and the Struggle for Freedom in the South."

While the *New York Times*, clearly no mean player in the news media business, received some income for running this full-page of advertising matter, it paid a far heavier price in the cost of subsequent litigation.[1] This plea for help in overcoming the final hurdle between good words and good practice became a First Amendment battleground in its own right — reaching its final argument before the United States Supreme Court on 6 January 1964 as the case of *New York Times Company, Petitioner, v. L. B. Sullivan*. Nine weeks later, on 9 March 1964, the court concluded its opinion by citing the case of John Peter Zenger in handing down its unanimous decision in favor of a free press.

SUMMARY

The present action for libel was brought in the Circuit Court of Montgomery County, Alabama, by a city commissioner of public affairs whose duties included supervision of the police department; the action was brought against the *New York Times* for publication of a paid advertisement describing the maltreatment in the city of Negro students protesting segregation, and against four individuals whose names, among others, appeared in the advertisement. The jury awarded plaintiff damages of $500,000 against all defendants, and the judgement on the verdict was affirmed by the Supreme Court of Alabama (273 Ala 656, 144 So 2d 25) on the grounds that the statements in the advertisement were libelous per se, false, and not privileged; the defendants constitutional objections were rejected on the ground that the First Amendment does not protect libelous publications.

On writs of certiorari, the Supreme Court of the United States reversed the judgement below and remanded the case to the Alabama Supreme Court. In an opinion by BRENNAN, J., expressing the views of six members of the Court, it was held that (1) the rule of law applied by the Alabama courts was constitutionally deficient for failure to provide the safeguards for freedom of speech and press that are required by the constitutional guaranty in a libel action brought by a public official against critics of his official conduct, and in particular, for failure to provide a qualified privilege for honest misstatements of fact, defeasible only upon a showing of actual malice; and (2) under the proper standards the evidence presented in the case was constitutionally insufficient to support the judgement for the plaintiff.

BLACK, J., joined by DOUGLAS, J., and GOLDBERG, J., joined by DOUGLAS, J., concurred in the result in separate opinions. The concurring opinions expressed the view that the constitutional guaranty of free speech and press afforded the defendants an absolute, unconditional privilege to publish their criticism of official conduct.[2]

In some ways, the trial of the *New York Times* and the four individual defendants was a replay of the trial of John Peter Zenger. A few errors of fact in the advertisement were noted, but the Supreme Court found them to be immaterial,[3] noting that "The trial judge submitted the case to the jury under instructions that the statements in the advertisement were 'libelous per se' and were not privileged, so that petitioners might be held liable if the jury found that they had published the advertisement and that the statements were made 'of and concerning' respondent [Commissioner L. B. ("Bull") Sullivan[4]]. The trial jury had thus been instructed — in language very reminiscent of that used by DeLancey — that, because the statements were libelous per se, "the law ... implies legal injury from the bare fact of publication itself...," falsity and malice are presumed" and "punitive damages may be awarded by the jury even though the amount of actual damages is neither found nor shown."

In affirming the judgement, the Supreme Court of Alabama sustained the trial judge's rulings and instructions in all respects. It held that "where the words published tend to injure a person libeled by them in his reputation, profession, trade or business, or charge him with an indictable offense, or tend to bring the individual into public contempt," they are "libelous per se."

In its sharp reversal of the Alabama Supreme Court's action, Justice

Brennan's opinion made a number of observations on behalf of the majority (the concurring opinions, quoted in summary above, were even stronger in their defense of a free press):

> The publication here was not a "commercial" advertisement.... It communicated information, expressed opinion, recited grievances, protested claimed abuses, and sought financial support on behalf of a movement whose existence and objectives are matters of the highest public interest and concern.... Any other conclusion would ... be to shackle the First Amendment in its attempt to secure "the widest possible dissemination of information from diverse and antagonistic sources." To avoid placing such a handicap upon the freedoms of expression, we hold that if the allegedly libelous statements would otherwise be constitutionally protected from the present judgement, they do not forfeit that protection because they were published in the form of a paid advertisement.

Citing a number of its own earlier decisions and references[5]— all reminiscent of those arguments used by Andrew Hamilton, the Supreme Court noted in unusually strong terms that it "retains and exercises authority to nullify action which encroaches on freedom of utterance under the guise of punishing libel" for "public men, are, as it were, public property," and "discussion cannot be denied and the right, as well as the duty, of criticism must not be stifled." Elsewhere the Court pronounced the dictum "It is a prized American privilege to speak one's mind, although not always with perfect good taste, on all public institutions...." "The First Amendment," said Judge Learned Hand, "presupposes that right conclusions are more likely to be gathered out of a multitude of tongues, than through any kind of authoritative selection. To many that is, and always will be, folly; but we have staked upon it our all." Quoting from Justice Louis Brandeis, Justice Brennan continued for the majority opinion:

> Those who won our independence believed ... that public discussion is a political duty; and that this should be a fundamental principle of the American government. They recognized the risks to which all human institutions are subject. But they knew that order cannot be secured merely through fear of punishment for its infraction; that it is hazardous to discourage thought, hope and imagination; that fear breeds repression; that repression breeds hate; that hate menaces stable government; that the path of safety lies in the opportunity to discuss freely supposed grievances and

proposed remedies; and that the fitting remedy for evil counsels is good ones. Believing in the power of reason as applied through public discussion, they eschewed silence coerced by law — the argument of force in its worst form. Recognizing the occasional tyrannies of governing majorities, they amended the Constitution so that free speech and assembly should be guaranteed."

And from James Madison, the foremost drafter of the American Constitution Brennan took these words: "'Some degree of abuse is inseparable from the proper use of everything; and in no instance is this more true than in that of the press.'" The Court also cited its own decision in the case of *Cantwell v. Connecticut*: "In the realm of religious faith, and in that of political belief, sharp differences arise. In both fields the tenets of one man may seem the rankest error to his neighbor. To persuade others to his own point of view, the pleader, as we know, at times, resorts to exaggeration, to vilification of men who have been, or are, prominent in church or state, and even to false statement. But the people of this nation have ordained in the light of history, that, in spite of the probability of excesses and abuses, these liberties are, in the long view, essential to enlightened opinion and right conduct on the part of citizens of a democracy."

In a decision bedecked with so many notations regarding the necessity for protection of the First Amendment freedoms, it is hard to select the most fitting to illustrate the longevity of those which were first uttered in this land of freedom by Andrew Hamilton. Justices Black and Douglas, in their concurring opinions saw through all the detail to a stark reality; they voted to reverse

> ... exclusively on the ground that the *Times* and the individual defendants had an absolute, unconditional constitutional right to publish in the *Times* advertisement their criticisms of the Montgomery agencies and officials. I do not base my vote to reverse on any failure to prove that these individual defendants signed the advertisement or that their criticism of the Police Department was aimed at the plaintiff Sullivan, who was then the Montgomery City Commissioner having supervision of the city's police; for present purposes I assume these things were proved. Nor is my reason for reversal the size of the half-million-dollar judgement, large as it is. If Alabama has constitutional power to use its civil libel law to impose damages on the press for criticizing the way public officials perform or fail to perform their duties, I know of no provision in the Federal Constitution which either expressly or impliedly bars the State from fixing the amount of damages.

The half-million-dollar verdict does give dramatic proof, however, that state libel laws threaten the very existence of an American press virile enough to publish unpopular views on public affairs and bold enough to criticize the conduct of public officials. The factual background of this case emphasizes the imminence and enormity of that threat. One of the acute and highly emotional issues in this country arises out of efforts of many people, even including some public officials, to continue state-commanded segregation of races in the public schools and other public places, despite our several holdings that such a state practice is forbidden by the Fourteenth Amendment. Montgomery is one of the localities in which wide-spread hostility to desegregation has been manifested. This hostility has sometimes extended itself to persons who favor desegregation, particularly to so-called "outside agitators," a term which can be made to fit papers like the *Times*, which is published in New York. The scarcity of testimony to show that Commissioner Sullivan suffered any actual damages at all suggests that these feelings of hostility had at least as much to do with rendition of this half-million-dollar verdict as did an appraisal of damages. Viewed realistically, this record lends support to an inference that instead of being damaged Commissioner Sullivan's political, social, and financial prestige has likely been enhanced by the *Times'* publication. Moreover, a second half-million-dollar libel verdict against the *Times* based on the same advertisement has already been awarded to another Commissioner.... There is no reason to believe that there are not more such huge verdicts lurking just around the corner for the Times or any other newspaper or broadcaster which might dare to criticize public officials.

In Justice Goldberg's concurring opinion, which Justice Douglas also shared, many of the same considerations were noted from a different angle, but he specifically harked back more than 229 years to Andrew Hamilton's exact words in defending John Peter Zenger:

> The opinion of the [Alabama] Court conclusively demonstrates the chilling effect of the Alabama libel laws on First Amendment freedoms in the area of race relations. The American Colonists were not willing, nor should we be, to take the risk that "*men who injure and oppress the people under their administration* [and] *provoke them to cry out and complain*" will also be empowered to "*make that very complaint the foundation for new oppressions and prosecutions.*"[6]

Afterword

Other than the messenger in folklore who lost his head for having fulfilled the unfortunate assignment of bringing bad news to the king, there have been a number of more authoritatively recorded spokespersons memorable for having reported the unwanted truth. Few of them were overwhelmingly popular in their time or place. However, almost all of them have been better served by history than by their contemporaries.

The story of John Peter Zenger is a typical illustration of this phenomenon. Clearly he left the scene of his, or Hamilton's, victory with no friends among Governor Cosby's clique — but such was hardly to be expected. His reward, if that is what it was, from the provincial assemblies of New York and New Jersey did not hold up very long or very well. And his *New York Weekly Journal*, regardless of its publisher's heroism in hindsight, survived him by only a few years — hardly a dynastic endeavor that made a lasting public impression. Only in modern schools of journalism is his name recalled with reverence, but even among most of their graduates it is soon forgotten in the crush of everyday issues. Only at the University of Arizona, across the continent from the scene of Zenger's sacrifice, is his name memorialized in a periodic award for courageous journalism in the face of official hostility.

One should also note that those of us who are proud of our Americanism all carry a good measure of nonconformism in our genes. We are a nation of malcontents and misfits, descended from those who for one reason or another were sufficiently unwanted, unfit, unrewarded or unpopular that they felt it better to endure the trials of immigration or civil protest to secure the unique rights guaranteed by the Constitution.

For all of his landmark status, Zenger has been treated poorly by historians generally. This has not come about because of malice, but rather because of ignorance, and in some ways it conveys his ultimate tribute. Zenger's place in history is little appreciated precisely because the right of free expression, which his trial and vindication brought to the rest of humanity, is so taken as God–given in modern democratic societies that few persons stop to think what life might be like if they were *not* able to communicate what they honestly believe is truth.

APPENDIX A
American Bill of Rights

I. Congress shall make no law respecting an establishment of religion, or prohibiting the free exercise thereof; or abridging the freedom of speech, or of the press, or the right of the people peaceably to assemble, and to petition the Government for a redress of grievances.

II. A well regulated militia, being necessary to the security of a free State, the right of the people to keep and bear Arms, shall not be infringed.

III. No Soldier shall, in time of peace be quartered in any house, without the consent of the Owner, nor in time of war, but in a manner prescribed by law.

IV. The right of the people to be secure in their persons, houses, papers and effects, against unreasonable searches and seizures, shall not be violated, and no Warrants shall issue, but upon probably cause, supported by Oath or affirmation, and particularly describing the place to be searched, and the person or things to be seized.

V. No person shall be held to answer for a capital, or otherwise infamous crime, unless on a presentment or indictment of a Grand Jury, except in cases arising in the land or naval forces, or in the Militia, when in actual service in time of War or public danger; nor shall any person be subject for the same offense to be twice put in jeopardy of life or limb; nor shall be compelled in any criminal case to be a witness against himself, nor be deprived of life, liberty, or property, without due process of law; nor shall private property be taken for public use, without just compensation.

VI. In all criminal prosecutions, the accused shall enjoy the right to a speedy and public trial, by an impartial jury of the State and district wherein the crime shall have been committed, which district shall have been previously ascertained by law, and to be informed of the nature and cause of the accusation; to be confronted with the witnesses against him;

to have compulsory process for obtaining witnesses in his favor, and to have the Assistance of Counsel for his defence.

VII. In Suits at common law, where the value in controversy shall exceed twenty dollars, the right of trial by jury shall be preserved, and no fact tried by a jury, shall be otherwise re-examined in any Court of the United States, that according to the rules of the common law.

VIII. Excessive bail shall not be required, nor excessive fines imposed, nor cruel and unusual punishments inflicted.

IX. The enumeration in the Constitution, of certain rights, shall not be construed to deny or disparage others retained by the people.

X. The powers not delegated to the United States by the Constitution, nor prohibited to it by the States, are reserved to the States respectively, or to the people.

* * * *

This Bill of Rights was adopted by the Congress on 25 September 1789, and promptly submitted to the states for their approval. New Jersey's came within two months, on 20 November, followed by Maryland on 19 December; North Carolina on 22 December; South Carolina on 19 January 1790; New Hampshire on 25 January; Delaware on 28 January; Pennsylvania on 10 March; Rhode Island on 15 June; New York on 27 October 1790; Vermont on 3 November 1791 and Virginia on 15 December, on which date these amendments became the law of the land.

Worthy of note is the fact that it was not until the spring of 1939 that the legislatures of Massachusetts, Georgia and Connecticut got around to formally voting approval of the rights their citizens had enjoyed for almost one hundred fifty years.

Since the "Civil War Amendments" had great bearing on subsequent decisions relating to freedom of speech, their text follows. All three contained a final section empowering Congress to enforce the article by appropriate legislation.

XIII. Neither slavery nor involuntary servitude, except as a punishment for crime whereof the party shall have been duly convicted, shall exist within the United States, or any place subject to their jurisdiction. (Ratified on 28 July 1865)

XIV. All persons born or naturalized in the United States, and subject to the jurisdiction thereof, are citizens of the United States and of the State wherein they reside. No state shall make or enforce any law which shall abridge the privileges or immunities of citizens of the United States; nor shall any State deprive any person of life, liberty, or property, without due process of law; nor deny to any person within its jurisdiction the equal protection of the laws.

Representatives shall be apportioned among the several states according to their respective numbers, counting the whole number of persons in each State, excluding Indians not taxed. But when the right to vote at any election for the choice of electors for President and Vice President of the United States, Representatives in Congress, the Executive and Judicial officers of a State, or members of the Legislature thereof, is denied to any of the male inhabitants of such State being twenty-one years of age, and citizens of the United States, or in any way abridged, except for participation in rebellion or other crime, the basis of representation therein shall be reduced in the proportion which the number of such male citizens shall bear to the whole number of male citizens twenty-one years of age in such State.

No person shall be a Senator or Representative in Congress, or elector of President and Vice President, or hold any office, civil or military, under the United States, or under any State, who, having previously taken an oath, as a member of Congress, or as an officer of the United States, or as a member of any State legislature, or as an executive of judicial officer of any State, to support the Constitution of the United States, shall have engaged in insurrection or rebellion against the same, or given aid and comfort to the enemies thereof. But Congress may, by vote of two-thirds of each House, remove such disability.

The validity of the public debt of the United States, authorized by law, including debts incurred for payment of pensions and bounties for services in suppression insurrection or rebellion, shall not be questioned. But neither the United States nor any State shall assume or pay any debt or obligation incurred in aid of insurrection or rebellion against the United States, or any claim for the loss or emancipation of any slave, but all such debts, obligations and claims shall be held illegal and void. (Ratified on 28 July 1865)

XV. The right of citizens of the United States to vote shall not be denied or abridged by the United States or by any State on account of race, color, or previous condition of servitude. (Ratified on 30 March 1870)

APPENDIX B
English Bill of Rights: An Act Declaring the Rights and Liberties of the Subject and Settling the Succession of the Crown
1689

Whereas the Lords Spiritual and Temporal and Commons assembled at Westminster, lawfully, fully and freely representing all the estates of the people of this realm, did upon the thirteenth day of February in the year of our Lord one thousand six hundred eighty-eight[1] present unto their Majesties, then called and known by the names and style of William and Mary, prince and princess of Orange, being present in their proper persons, a certain declaration in writing made by the said Lords and Commons in the words following, viz.:

Whereas the late King James the Second, by the assistance of divers evil counsellors, judges and ministers employed by him, did endeavour to subvert and extirpate the Protestant religion and the laws and liberties of this kingdom;

By assuming and exercising a power of dispensing with and suspending of laws and the execution of laws without consent of Parliament;

By committing and prosecuting divers worthy prelates for humbly petitioning to be excused from concurring to the said assumed power;

By issuing and causing to be executed a commission under the great seal for erecting a court called the Court of Commissioners for Ecclesiastical Causes;

By levying money for and to the use of the Crown by pretence of prerogative for other time and in other manner than the same was granted by Parliament;

By raising and keeping a standing army within this kingdom in time of peace without consent of Parliament, and quartering soldiers contrary to law;

By causing several good subjects being Protestants to be disarmed at the same time when papists were both armed and employed contrary to law;

By violating the freedom of election of members to serve in Parliament;

By prosecutions in the Court of King's Bench for matters and causes cognizable only in Parliament, and by divers other arbitrary and illegal courses;

And whereas of late years partial corrupt and unqualified persons have been returned and served on juries in trials, and particularly divers jurors in trials for high treason which were not freeholders;

And excessive bail hath been required of persons committed in criminal cases to elude the benefit of the laws made for the liberty of the subjects;

And excessive fines have been imposed;

And illegal and cruel punishments inflicted;

And several grants and promises made of fines and forfeitures before any conviction or judgment against the persons upon whom the same were to be levied;

All which are utterly and directly contrary to the known laws and statutes and freedom of this realm;

And whereas the said late King James the Second having abdicated the government and the throne being thereby vacant, his Highness the prince of Orange (whom it hath pleased Almighty God to make the glorious instrument of delivering this kingdom from popery and arbitrary power) did (by the advice of the Lords Spiritual and Temporal and divers principal persons of the Commons) cause letters to be written to the Lords Spiritual and Temporal being Protestants, and other letters to the several counties, cities, universities, boroughs and cinque ports, for the choosing of such persons to represent them as were of right to be sent to Parliament to meet and sit at Westminster upon the two and twentieth day of January in this year one thousand six hundred eighty and eight, in order to such an establishment as that their religion, laws and liberties might not again be in danger of being subverted, upon which letters elections having been accordingly made;

And thereupon the said Lords Spiritual and Temporal and Commons, pursuant to their respective letters and elections, being now assembled in a full and free representative of this nation, taking into their most serious consideration the best means for attaining the ends aforesaid, do in the first place (as their ancestors in like case have usually done) for the vindicating and asserting their ancient rights and liberties declare

That the pretended power of suspending of laws or the execution of laws by regal authority without consent of Parliament is illegal;

That the pretended power of dispensing with laws or the execution of laws by regal authority, as it hath been assumed and exercised of late, is illegal;

That the commission for erecting the late Court of Commissioners for Ecclesiastical Causes, and all other commissions and courts of like nature, are illegal and pernicious;

That levying money for or to the use of the Crown by pretense of prerogative, without grant of Parliament, for longer time, or in other manner than the same is or shall be granted, is illegal;

That it is the right of the subjects to petition the king, and all commitments and prosecutions for such petitioning are illegal;

That the raising or keeping a standing army within the kingdom in time of peace, unless it be with consent of Parliament, is against law;

That the subjects which are Protestants may have arms for their defence suitable to their conditions and as allowed by law;

That election of members of Parliament ought to be free;

That the freedom of speech and debates or proceedings in Parliament ought not to be impeached or questioned in any court or place out of Parliament;

That excessive bail ought not to be required, nor excessive fines imposed, nor cruel and unusual punishments inflicted;

That jurors ought to be duly impanelled and returned, and jurors which pass upon men in trials for high treason ought to be freeholders;

That all grants and promises of fines and forfeitures of particular persons before conviction are illegal and void;

And that for redress of all grievances, and for the amending, strengthening and preserving of the laws, Parliaments ought to be held frequently.

And they do claim, demand and insist upon all and singular the premises as their undoubted rights and liberties, and that no declarations, judgments, doings or proceedings to the prejudice of the people in any of the said premises ought in any wise to be drawn hereafter into consequence or example; to which demand of their rights they are particularly encouraged by the declaration of his Highness the prince of Orange as being the only means for obtaining a full redress and remedy therein. Having therefore an entire confidence that his said Highness the prince of Orange will perfect the deliverance so far advanced by him, and will still preserve them from the violation of their rights which they have here asserted, and from all other attempts upon their religion, rights and liberties, the said Lords Spiritual and Temporal and Commons assembled at Westminster do resolve that William and Mary, prince and princess of Orange, be and be declared king and queen of England, France and Ireland and the dominions thereunto belonging, to hold the crown and royal dignity of the said kingdoms and dominions to them, the said prince and princess, during their lives and the life of the survivor of them, and that the sole and full exercise of the regal power be only in and executed by the said prince of Orange in the names of the said prince and princess during their joint lives, and after their deceases the said crown and royal dignity of the said kingdoms and dominions to be to the heirs of the body of the said princess, and for default of such issue to the Princess Anne of Denmark and the heirs of her body, and for default of such issue to the heirs of the body of the said prince of Orange. And the Lords Spiritual and Temporal and Commons do pray the said prince and princess to accept the same accordingly.

And that the oaths hereafter mentioned be taken by all persons of whom the oaths of allegiance and supremacy might be required by law, instead of them; and that the said oaths of allegiance and supremacy be abrogated.

I, A.B., do sincerely promise and swear that I will be faithful and bear true allegiance to their Majesties King William and Queen Mary. So help me God.

I, A.B., do swear that I do from my heart abhor, detest and abjure as impious and heretical this damnable doctrine and position, that princes excommunicated or deprived by the Pope or any authority of the see of Rome may be deposed or murdered by their subjects or any other whatsoever. And I do declare that no foreign prince, person, prelate, state or potentate hath or ought to have any jurisdiction, power, superiority, pre-eminence or authority, ecclesiastical or spiritual, within this realm. So help me God.

Upon which their said Majesties did accept the crown and royal dignity of the kingdoms of England, France and Ireland, and the dominions thereunto belonging, according to the resolution and desire of the said Lords and Commons contained in the said declaration. And thereupon their Majesties were pleased that the said Lords Spiritual and Temporal and Commons being the two Houses of Parliament, should continue to sit, and with their Majesties' royal concurrence make effectual provision for the settlement of the religion, laws and liberties of this kingdom, so that the same for the future might not be in danger again of being subverted, to which the said Lords Spiritual and Temporal and Commons did agree, and proceed to act accordingly. Now, in pursuance of the premises the said Lords Spiritual and Temporal and Commons in Parliament assembled, for the ratifying, confirming and establishing the said declaration and the articles, clauses, matters and things therein contained by the force of a law made in due form by authority of Parliament, do pray that it may be declared and enacted that all and singular the rights and liberties asserted and claimed in the said declaration are the true, ancient and indubitable rights and liberties of the people of this kingdom, and so shall be esteemed, allowed, adjudged, deemed and taken to be; and that all and every the particulars aforesaid shall be firmly and strictly holden and observed as they are expressed in the said declaration, and all officers and ministers whatsoever shall serve their Majesties and their successors according to the same in all times to come. And the said Lords Spiritual and Temporal and Commons, seriously considering how it hath pleased Almighty God in his marvelous providence and merciful goodness to this nation to provide and preserve their said Majesties royal persons most happily to reign over us upon the throne of their ancestors, for which they render unto him from the bottom of their hearts their humblest thanks and praises, do truly, firmly, assuredly and in the sincerity of their hearts think, and do hereby recognize, acknowledge and declare, that King James the Second having abdicated the government, and their Majesties having accepted the crown and royal dignity as aforesaid, their said Majesties did become, were, are and of right ought to be by the laws of this realm our sovereign liege lord and lady, king and queen of England, France and Ireland and the dominions thereunto belonging, in and to whose princely persons the royal state, crown and dignity of the said realms with all honours, styles, titles, regalities, prerogatives, powers, jurisdictions and authorities to the same belonging and appertaining are most fully, rightfully and entirely invested and incorporated, united and annexed. And for preventing all questions and divisions in this realm by reason of any pretended titles to the crown, and for preserving a certainty in the succession thereof, in and upon which the unity, peace, tranquillity and safety of this nation doth under God wholly consist and depend, the said Lords Spiritual and Temporal and Commons do beseech their Majesties that it may be enacted, established and declared, that the crown and regal government of the said kingdoms and dominions, with all and singular the premises thereunto belonging and appertaining, shall be and continue to their said Majesties and the survivor of them during their lives and the life of the survivor of them, and that the entire, perfect and full exercise of the regal power and government be only in and executed by his Majesty in the names of both their Majesties during their joint lives; and after their deceases the said crown and premises shall be and remain to the heirs of the body of her Majesty, and for default of such issue to her Royal Highness the Princess Anne of Denmark and the heirs of her body, and for default of such issue to the heirs of the body of his said Majesty;[2] and thereunto the said Lords Spiritual and Temporal and Commons do in the name of all the people aforesaid most humbly and faithfully submit themselves, their heirs and posterities for ever, and do faithfully promise that they will stand to, maintain and defend their said Majesties, and also the limitation and succession of the crown herein specified and contained, to the utmost of their powers with their lives and estates against all persons whatsoever that shall attempt anything to the contrary. And whereas it hath been found by experience that it is inconsistent with the safety and welfare of this Protestant kingdom to be governed by a popish prince, or by any king or queen marrying a papist, the said Lords Spiritual and Temporal and Commons do further pray that it may be enacted, that all and every person and persons that is, are or shall be reconciled to or shall hold communion with the see or Church of Rome, or shall profess the popish religions or shall marry a papist, shall be excluded and be for ever incapable to inherit, possess or enjoy the crown and government of this realm and Ireland and the dominions thereunto belonging or any part of the same, or to have, use or exercise any regal power, authority or jurisdiction within the same; and in all and every such case or cases the people of these realms shall be and are hereby absolved of their allegiance; and the said crown and government shall from time to time descend to and be enjoyed by such person or persons being Protestants as should have inherited and enjoyed the same in case the said person or persons so reconciled, holding communion or professing or marrying as aforesaid were naturally dead; and that every king and queen of this realm who at any time hereafter shall come to and succeed in the imperial crown of this kingdom shall on the first dan of the meeting of the first Parliament next after his or her coming to the crown, sitting in his or her throne in the House of Peers in the presence of the Lords and Commons therein assembled or at his or her coronation before such person or persons who shall administer the coronation oath to him or her at the time of his or her taking the said oath (which shall first happen), make, subscribe and audibly repeat the declaration mentioned in the statute made in the thirtieth year of the reign of King Charles the Second entituled, *An Act for the more effectual preserving the king's person and government by disabling papists from sitting in either House of Parliament.* But if it shall happen that such king or queen upon his or her succession to the crown of this realm shall be under the age of twelve years, then every such king or queen shall make, subscribe and audibly repeat the said declaration at his or her coronation or the first day of the meeting of the first Parliament as aforesaid which shall first happen after such king or queen shall have attained the said age of twelve years. All which their Majesties are contented and pleased shall be declared, enacted and established by authority of this present Parliament, and shall stand remain and be the law of this realm for ever; and the same are by their said Majesties, by and Faith the advice and consent of the Lords Spiritual and Temporal and Commons in Parliament assembled and by the authority of the same, declared, enacted and established accordingly.

II. And be it further declared and enacted by the authority aforesaid that from and after this present session of Parliament no dispensation be *non obstante*[3] of or to any statute or any part thereof shall be allowed, but that the same shall be held void and of no effect, except a dispensation be allowed of in such statute, and except in such cases as shall be specially provided for by one or more bill or bills to be passed during this present session of Parliament.

III. Provided that no charter or grant or pardon granted before the three and twentieth day of October in the year of our Lord one thousand six hundred eighty-nine shall be any Bass impeached or invalidated by this Act, but that the same shall be and remain of the same force and effect in law and no other than as if this Act had never been made.

APPENDIX C
Declaration of Independence in Congress, July 4, 1776: The Unanimous Declaration of the Thirteen United States of America

When in the Course of human events, it becomes necessary for one people to dissolve the political bands which have connected them with another, and to assume among the powers of the earth, the separate and equal station to which the Laws of Nature and of Nature's God entitle them, a decent respect to the opinions of mankind requires that they should declare the causes which impel them to the separation.

We hold these truths to be self-evident, that all men are created equal, that they are endowed by their Creator with certain unalienable Rights, that among these are Life, Liberty and the pursuit of Happiness. That to secure these rights, Governments are instituted among Men, deriving their just powers from the consent of the governed, That whenever any Form of Government becomes destructive of these ends, it is the Right of the People to alter or to abolish it, and to institute new Government, laying its foundation on such principles and organizing its powers in such form, as to them shall seem most likely to effect their Safety and Happiness.

Prudence, indeed, will dictate that Governments long established should not be changed for light and transient causes; and accordingly all experience hath shown, that mankind are more disposed to suffer, while evils are sufferable, than to right themselves by abolishing the forms to which they are accustomed. But when a long train of abuses and usurpations, pursuing invariably the same Object evinces a design to reduce them under absolute Despotism, it is their right, it is their duty, to throw off such Government, and to provide new Guards for their future security.

Such has been the patient sufferance of these Colonies; and such is now the necessity which constrains them to alter their former Systems of Government.

The history of the present King of Great Britain is a history of repeated injuries and usurpations, all having in direct object the establishment of an absolute Tyranny over these States. To prove this let Facts be submitted to a candid world.

He has refused his Assent to Laws, the most wholesome and necessary for the public good.

He has forbidden his Governors to pass Laws of immediate and pressing importance, unless suspended in their operation till his Assent should be obtained; and when so suspended, he has utterly neglected to attend to them.

He has refused to pass other Laws for the accommodation of large districts of people, unless those people would relinquish the right of Representation in the Legislature, a right inestimable to them and formidable to tyrants only.

He has called together legislative bodies at places unusual, uncomfortable, and distant from the depository of their public Records, for the sole purpose of fatiguing them into compliance with his measures.

He has dissolved Representative Houses repeatedly, for opposing with manly firmness his invasions on the rights of the people.

He has refused for a long time, after such dissolutions, to cause others to be elected; whereby the Legislative powers, incapable of Annihilation have returned to the People at large for their exercise; the State remaining in the mean time exposed to all the dangers of invasion from without, and convulsions within.

He has endeavoured to prevent the population of these States; for that purpose obstructing the Laws for Naturalization of Foreigners; refusing to pass others to encourage their migration hither, and raising the conditions of new Appropriations of Lands.

He has obstructed the Administration of Justice, by refusing his Assent to Laws for establishing Judiciary powers.

He has made judges dependent on his Will alone, for the tenure of their offices, and the amount and payment of their salaries.

He has erected a multitude of New Offices, and sent hither swarms of Officers to harrass our people, and eat out their substance.

He has kept among us, in times of peace, Standing Armies, without the Consent of our legislatures.

He has affected to render the Military independent of and superior to the Civil power.

He has combined with others to subject us to a jurisdiction foreign to our constitution, and unacknowledged by our laws; giving his Assent to their Acts of pretended Legislation:

For quartering large bodies of armed troops among us:

For protecting them, by a mock Trial, from punishment for any Murders which they should commit on the Inhabitants of these States:

For cutting off our Trade with all parts of the world:

For imposing Taxes on us without our Consent:

For depriving us in many cases, of the benefits of Trial by Jury:

For transporting us beyond Seas to be tried for pretended offences:

For abolishing the free System of English Laws in a neighbouring Province, establishing therein an Arbitrary government, and enlarging its Boundaries so as to render it at once an example and fit instrument for introducing the same absolute rule into these Colonies:

For taking away our Charters, abolishing our most valuable Laws, and altering fundamentally the Forms of our Governments:

For suspending our own Legislatures, and declaring themselves invested with power to legislate for us in all cases whatsoever.

He has abdicated Government here, by declaring us out of his Protection and waging War against us.

He has plundered our seas, ravaged our Coasts, burnt our towns, and destroyed the lives of our people.

He is at this time transporting large Armies of foreign Mercenaries to compleat the works of death, desolation and tyranny, already begun with circumstances of Cruelty & perfidy scarcely paralleled in the most barbarous ages, and totally unworthy the Head of a civilized nation.

He has constrained our fellow Citizens taken Captive on the high Seas to bear Arms against their Country, to become the executioners of their friends and Brethren, or to fall themselves by their Hands.

He has excited domestic insurrections amongst us, and has endeavoured to bring on the inhabitants of our frontiers, the merciless Indian Savages, whose known rule of warfare, is an undistinguished destruction of all ages, sexes and conditions.

In every stage of these Oppressions We have Petitioned for Redress in the most humble terms: Our repeated Petitions have been answered only by repeated injury.

A Prince, whose character is thus marked by every act which may define a Tyrant, is unfit to be the ruler of a free people. Nor have We been wanting in attentions to our Brittish brethren. We have warned them from time to time of attempts by their legislature to extend an unwarrantable jurisdiction over us. We have reminded them of the circumstances of our emigration and settlement here. We have appealed to their native justice and magnanimity, and we have conjured them by the ties of our common kindred to disavow these usurpations, which, would inevitably interrupt our connections and correspondence. They too have been deaf to the voice of justice and of consanguinity. We must, therefore, acquiesce in the necessity, which denounces our Separation, and hold them, as we hold the rest of mankind. Enemies in War, in Peace Friends.

We, therefore, the Representatives of the United States of America, in General Congress, Assembled, appealing to the Supreme Judge of the world for the rectitude of our intentions, do, in the Name, and by Authority of the good People of these Colonies, solemnly publish and declare, That these United Colonies are, and of Right ought to be Free and Independent States; that they are Absolved from all Allegiance to the British Crown, and that all political connection between them and the State of Great Britain, is and ought to be totally dissolved; and that as Free and Independent States, they have full Power to levy War, conclude Peace, contract Alliances, establish Commerce, and to do all other Acts and Things which Independent States may of right do.—And for the support of this Declaration, with a firm reliance on the protection of Divine Providence, we mutually pledge to each other our Lives, our Fortunes and our sacred Honor.

John Hancock

New Hampshire
Josiah Bartlett
Wm. Whipple
Matthew Thornton

Massachusetts Bay
Saml. Adams
John Adams
Robt. Treat Paine
Elbridge Gerry

Rhode Island
Step. Hopkins
William Ellery

Connecticut
Roger Sherman
Sam'el Huntington
Wm. Williams
Oliver Wolcott

New York
Wm. Floyd
Phil. Livingston
Frans. Lewis
Lewis Morris

Maryland
Samuel Chase
Wm. Paca
Thos. Stone
Charles Carroll of Carrollton

Virginia
George Wythe

New Jersey
Richd. Stockton
Jno. Witherspoon
Fras. Hopkinson
John Hart
Abra. Clark

Pennsylvania
Robt. Morris
Benjamin Rush
Benja. Franklin
John Morton
Geo. Clymer
Jas. Smith
Geo. Taylor
James Wilson
Geo. Ross

Delaware

Caesar Rodney
Geo. Read
Tho. M'Kean

North Carolina

Wm. Hooper
Joseph Hewes
John Penn

South Carolina

Edward Rutledge
Thos. Heyward, Junr.
Thomas Lynch, Junr.
Arthur Middleton

Georgia

Richard Henry Lee
Th. Jefferson
Benja. Harrison
Ths. Nelson, Jr.
Francis Lightfoot Lee
Carter Braxton
Button Gwinnett
Lyman Hall
Geo. Walton

APPENDIX D
Declaration of the Rights of Man and of the Citizen (Déclaration des Droits de l'Homme et du Citoyen)

Adopted by the National Assembly of France, 26 August 1789[1]

This document was largely drafted by the Abbé Emmanuel-Joseph Sieyès (1748–1836) a sometime churchman and constitutional theorist, whose contemporaries said that he could draft a constitution on an hour's notice. His principal theoretical basis was the premise that fundamental control of government should rest in the French Third[2] Estate, a bit closer to the people who numbered some 24,000,000 at the time this document was adopted.

Sieyès voted for the execution of King Louis XVI in January 1793, but withdrew from public affairs when the Jacobins seized control six months later and began the Reign of Terror. Returning to power a few years later he aided in the military coup d'etat that brought Napoleon Bonaparte to power. After the Bourbon restoration in 1815, he was banished as a regicide, but ultimately returned to Paris in 1830.

PREAMBLE

The representatives of the French people, formed into a National Assembly, considering ignorance, forgetfulness or contempt of the rights of man to be the only causes of public misfortunes and the corruption of Governments, have resolved to set forth, in a solemn Declaration, the natural, unalienable and sacred rights of man, to the end that this Declaration, constantly present to all members of the body politic, may remind them unceasingly of their rights and duties; to the end that the acts of the legislative power and those of the executive power, since they may be continually compared with the aim of every political institution, may thereby be the more respected; to the end that the demands of the citizens, founded henceforth on simple and uncontestable principles, may always be directed toward maintenance of the Constitution and the happiness of all.

In consequence whereof, the National Assembly recognizes and declares, in the presence and under the auspices of the Supreme Being, the following Rights of Man and of the Citizen.

ARTICLE FIRST — Men are born and remain free and equal in rights. Social distinctions may be based only on considerations of the common good.

ARTICLE 2 — The aim of every political association is the preservation of the natural and imprescriptible rights of man. These rights are Liberty, Property, Safety and Resistance to Oppression.

ARTICLE 3 — Liberty consists in being able to do anything that does not harm others: thus, the exercise of the natural rights of every man has no bounds other than those that ensure to the other members of society the enjoyment of these same rights. These bounds may be determined only by Law.

ARTICLE 4 — The Law has the right to forbid only those actions that are injurious to society. Nothing that is not forbidden by Law may be hindered, and no one may be compelled to do what the Law does not ordain.

ARTICLE 6 — The Law is the expression of the general will. All citizens have the right to take part, personally or through their representatives, in its making. It must be the same for all, whether it protects or punishes. All citizens, being equal in its eyes, shall be equally eligible to all high offices, public positions and employments, according to their ability, and without other distinction that of their virtues and talents.

ARTICLE 7 — No man may be accused, arrested or detained except in the cases determined by the Law, and following the procedure that it has prescribed. Those who solicit, expedite, carry out, or cause to be carried out arbitrary orders must be punished; but any citizen summoned or apprehended by virtue of the Law, must give instant obedience; resistance makes him guilty.

ARTICLE 8 — The Law must prescribe only the punishments that are strictly and evidently necessary; and no one may be punished except by virtue of a Law drawn up and promulgated before the offense is committed, and legally applied.

ARTICLE 9 — As every man is presumed innocent until he has been declared guilty, if it should be considered necessary to arrest him, any undue harshness that is not required to secure his person must be severely curbed by Law.

ARTICLE 10 — No one may be disturbed on account of his opinions, even religious ones, as long as the manifestation of such opinion does not interfere with the established Law and Order.

ARTICLE 11—The free communication of ideas and of opinions is one of the most precious rights of man. Any citizen may therefore, speak, write and publish freely, except what is tantamount to the abuse of this liberty in the cases determined by Law.

ARTICLE 12 — To guarantee the Rights of Man and of the Citizen a public force is necessary; this force is therefore established for the benefit of all, and not for the particular use of those to whom it is entrusted.

ARTICLE 13 — For the maintenance of the public force, and for administrative expenses, a general tax is indispensable; it must be equally distributed among all citizens, in proportion to their ability to pay.

ARTICLE 14 — All citizens have the right to ascertain, by themselves, or through their representatives, the need for a public tax, to consent to it freely, to watch over its use, and to determine its proportion, basis, collection and duration.

ARTICLE 15 — Society has the right to ask a public official for an accounting of his administration.

ARTICLE 16 — Any society in which no provision is made for guaranteeing rights or for the separation of powers, has no Constitution.

ARTICLE 17 — Since the right to Property is inviolable and sacred, no one may be deprived thereof, unless public necessity, legally ascertained, obviously requires it, and just and prior indemnity has been paid.

Notes

Chapter I

1. Their official title was "Count Palatine of the Rhine; Arch-Treasurer and Elector of the Empire; Duke of Bavaria, Juliers, Cleves and Berg; Count of Veldentz, Spanheim, Marck, Ravensberg and Moeurs; Lord of Ravenstein."

2. When Pope Innocent X was informed of the terms of the Peace of Westphalia, he issued a Bull *Zelo domus Dei* (20 November 1648) in which he pronounced it "ipso iure nulla, irrita, invalida, iniqua, iniusta, damnata, reprobata, inania, viribusque et effecta vacua, omnino fuisse, esse, et perpetua fore...." But it went into effect anyway.

3. This provision first appeared as a result of the Religious Peace of Augsburg in 1554. Settled at a diet in that city, it allowed each German prince to impose on his subjects the religion he had personally selected; it also permitted Lutheran princes to retain all the ecclesiastical estates they had acquired before 1552, but stripped of all lands and privileges any prelate who left the Church of Rome.

4. The Dutch had ceded Nieuw Netherland in 1664 at the conclusion of the first Dutch War, but had briefly recaptured it during the second Dutch War.

5. Palatines are not to be confused with Mennonites, the Anabaptist followers of Menno Simonszoon (1496–1561) and ancestors of the Pennsylvania "Dutch," though their origins in Teutonic central Europe and their reasons for leaving are similar.

6. This is a dozen kilometers upriver from the Brienzee and not far from the Aareschlucht, where Sherlock Holmes had his final encounter with the infamous Professor Moriarty.

7. Robert Hunter (d. 1734), a distinguished British soldier, was appointed governor of the combined colonies of New York and New Jersey, assuming office in 1710. One of the few successful and popular royal governors, he also instituted an overland postal service between Boston and New York — predecessor of later "Boston post roads." In 1727, he was reassigned as governor of Jamaica.

8. Bradford had been printing material for Governor Hyde (Lord Cornbury) as early as 1702.

9. Joseph Glover, a wealthy Puritan clergyman died at sea while bringing his press and materials to the New World. His estate became largely associated with Harvard College as a result of the marriage of his widow to president Henry Dunster early in 1654. Dunster, incidentally, lost his job later in the year because of his increasingly Baptist views, which were unacceptible to the overseers of the college.

10. George Keith (1638–1716), born in Peterhead, Scotland, was one of the original members of the Quaker movement. Appointed surveyor general of Pennsylvania in 1685, he later became critical of the failure of the Friends' leadership to adequately appreciate Christ. Ultimately disowned by them, he took Anglican orders in 1700 and continued his missionary work in America until 1704 when he returned to England.

11. Fletcher (d. 1703) was governor of New York and Pennsylvania from 1692 to 1697. He was deposed and sent home under arrest after being accused of making numerous fraudulent land deals and befriending several known pirates.

12. William Bradford had similarly sheltered Franklin, who trudged onward to Philadelphia in search of employment. He found it, unfortunately for his hosts, in working for Samuel Keimer, Philadelphia's "other" printer.

13. Harris (who flourished between 1763 and 1716), was a friend of Anthony Cooper, Lord Shaftesbury, and involved in the exposure of the "popish plot" with Titus Oates in 1679. He had published a paper in England but left the homeland in 1686, after the failure of Monmouth's revolution, and became official printer to the governor of Massachusetts in 1692. Returning to London in 1695, he published the *London Post* from 1696 to 1706.

14. Bradstreet was governor of all New England from 7 June 1689 to 17 May 1692. A lot of useful data on the politics of this period comes from the diary of Judge Samuel Sewall (1652–1730), a longtime jurist of the Bay colony and ultimately chief justice of the supreme judicial court. Among his greater distinctions was that of having confessed to error subsequent to his presiding over the famous witch trials of 1692 in Salem Village.

15. The exact language in one colonial governor's instructions read as follows: "Forasmuch as great inconvenience may arise by liberty of printing within our said territory under your government you are to provide by all necessary orders that no person keep any printing-press for printing, nor that any book pamphlet or other matter whatsoever be printed without your especial leave and license first obtained."

16. Harison, the appointee of Governor Cosby, was a two-timing land speculator in addition to his other faults. When he was faced with his record, he fled the colony back to England, where he died in obscurity.

17. Edgar A. Werner, *Civil List and Constitutional History of the Colony and State of New York* (Albany: Weed, Parson, 1888): 135–36.

18. Under the English rule, the governor was limited in his ability to dismiss recalcitrant members of the Council. But Peter Stuyvesant actually had soldiers evict members bodily, and in another instance he caned a councilor for opposing his will.

19. Giving credence to a more modern definition of the word "indifferent" than meant by Charles Hildeburn in his 1895 description of Zenger, this first issue was dated 5 October—a month wrong.

Chapter II

1. A lampoon with political significance.

2. Thomas (1750–1831) published the *Massachusetts Spy* in various locations after being chased out of Boston by the British. For his efforts he was rewarded with the postmastership of Worcester, Massachusetts, a position he held from 1775 to 1801. In 1812, he was a founder and first president of the American Antiquarian Society. Thomas was not, however, totally unbiased and had a strong streak of self-orientation.

3. Charles Swift Riche Hildeburn (1855–1901) wrote *Sketches of Printers and Printing in Colonial New York* in 1895. Three hundred seventy-five copies were printed by Dodd, Mead and Company.

4. Queen Anne's death in 1714 was seized upon as a rallying effort to prevent the Hanoverian succession. The disastrous battles of Preston and Sheriffmuir settled the matter quickly, however, leaving a number of Scots homeless and orphaned. After this debacle, the "Old Pretender," James Edward, retired from the fray and lived briefly in Avignon before migrating on to Rome.

5. The quotations in these paragraphs are from page 126 of *Murder, Piracy and Treason* by Raymond W. Postgate (London: 1949).

6. The *Dictionary of American Biography* sums up this governor's biography thus: "Cosby's correspondence shows him to have been devoid of statesmanship, seeking money and preferment."

7. The colonies represented at this conference—which had the sanction of London—were New Hampshire, Massachusetts, Connecticut, Rhode Island, Pennsylvania, Maryland and New York.

Smith's son, William, Jr., (1729–1793) remained loyal to King George III, was dispossessed in New York after the Revolution and became the chief justice of Upper Canada in 1786.

8. Morrisania (1697) was one of the six formally chartered "Westchester Manors" under a provision granted by Charles II. The others were Fordham (1671); Pelham (1687); Philipseburgh (1693); Van Cortlandt (1697)

and Scarsdale (1701). In an ironic twist, during the Revolutionary War, Morrisania was occupied by Lt. Col. James DeLancey, loyalist son of the presiding judge in Zenger's trial.

9. John Montgomerie (d. 1731), a native of Scotland, was the appointed governor prior to Cosby. He had died in office in mid–1731 during an epidemic of smallpox and was not replaced for more than a year.

10. Daily papers, while successful in London, were almost a century in the future in North America. Zenger's font and press, like all the others in the colonies, were made in England and exported overseas when English printers sought to upgrade their establishments.

11. The original church was a frame building only twenty-eight feet square, shingled on the outside and wainscotted within. It was replaced with a larger stone edifice some sixty years after the election.

12. Cooper's substantial personal dimensions soon became the butt of one of the *Journal*'s spurious ads.

13. The exact price put on the governor's good will is difficult to calculate at this distance in time. A pistole was a fairly common name for several coins issued in that era. The most common, however, was the gold double escudo, a Spanish coin minted between 1537 and 1847, known in England as a "doubloon." Other pistoles were issued by various German states, some with a value of 5 thaler.

14. Archaic form of "tablet."

15. This passage of the *New York Weekly Journal* is taken mostly from that given in *The Trial of Peter Zenger*, edited by Vincent Buranelli (New York: New York University Press, 1957).

Chapter III

1. The literature of classical studies, however, contains numerous learned articles on this topic, many of which illustrate both the successes and failures of those who spoke freely.

2. In more modern times Mikhail Gorbachev seems to have been a striking exception to this statement.

3. Every clergyman in the kingdom was forbidden to say mass in public, hear confessions, bury the dead, grant absolution, perform marriages or in general do any of the functions of the priesthood.

4. This was a procedure started by Henry II in 1166 whereby a person wrongfully dispossessed of land could seek to recover. This archaic process was finally abolished in 1833.

5. This long-dormant legal procedure allowed for the heir to recover from an interloper who took possession of a property in which the plaintiff's forebears had an interest.

6. This archaic legal procedure dealt with ecclesiastical benefices.

7. Fined except in accordance with existing statutory procedure.

8. Dispossessed of land rightfully held.

9. Charles II had dismissed the "Oxford" parliament in 1680 and had never called another. Thus the offenses charged were done as much by his brother as by James II.

10. These clauses largely rehashed of the language used in the 1678 Test Act and the 1679 Exclusion Bill (which failed of enactment), both of which were designed to ensure that "popery" never showed itself on the English throne in the future.

11. Trenchard (1662–1723) was educated at Trinity College, Dublin, and wrote initially on the impropriety of standing armies in times of peace. With Gordon, he published the *Independent Whig* from 20 January 1720, to 18 June 1721. On his deathbed, he urged the already widowed Gordon to marry his wife, Anne [Blackett]. And Gordon did.

12. The full text of this essay was also reprinted by Zenger in 1733 in an early issue of his *New York Weekly Journal*.

13. By now, this was Boston's third newspaper. It was published on Mondays and had to do without its editor until the General Court session was concluded — about one month later.

14. This philosophy reached its apogee under the ill-starred leadership of General Nivelle in his 1917 "Chemin des Dames" offensive.

Chapter IV

1. The Official Secrets and Defence of the Realm Acts still allow Her Majesty's government the power to prohibit publication under a variety of non-wartime conditions.

2. A. L. Smith, of Baliol College, in the six Ford Lectures of 1905 (Clarendon Press, 1913).

3. Some of these "perks" were significant and definite signs of worldliness. One "independent" monastery, Sempringham, had sixty-two advowsons (non-resident patronage appointments) at its disposal, most of which were dealt out at the dictation of Rome.

4. One such abbey still survives: Battle, founded by William I on the site of his victory over Harold, which became a private estate for a series of royal favorites until it became untenable due to decay. It was rescued in the early nineteenth century and rehabilitated as a girls' boarding school.

5. The Avignon "captivity" lasted from 1309 to 1378, and the "Great Schism" continued the "frenchification" of the Papacy until 1408.

6. James lived out his days as a dependent of Louis XIV, who had subsidized both him and his brother, Charles II, for many years; but he is buried in Rome.

7. Andros (1637–1714) was one of the most high-handed of all colonial governors. In 1688 James created him governor of a "dominion" consisting of all New England along with New York and New Jersey. However, when colonials in Boston under the leadership of Increase and Cotton Mather heard of James's overthrow in 1689, they put the unpopular governor in chains and sent him home. Somewhat rehabilitated and chastened under William and Mary, he returned in 1692 as governor of Virginia.

8. William's mother was a daughter of Charles I and his wife a daughter of James II, so they had quite legitimate claims to the succession, but both professed vigorous Protestantism and were thus quite acceptable to the assorted barons of Britain.

9. Though supposedly entitled to places in the House of Lords, most truly Irish barons were denied their seats as long as they adhered to the Church of Rome.

10. This language, appearing in Article V, Clause 5, of the Articles, was carried forward almost verbatim to Article I, Section 1, of the United States Constitution.

11. The proper name for the Massachusetts legislature is "The General Court," a term that reflects its dual origin in colonial times. In more recent years, its members have taken to calling themselves collectively "The Great and General Court," a term that is only occasionally verified by its actions.

12. The first United States census, in 1790, came up with a total population of 3,929,214, of whom 681,834 were Negro slaves. Indians did not count at all.

13. The Irish population of some 5,000,000 was one-third of the total in the British Isles and may have not been nearly as enthusiastic in aiding the suppression of colonial rebellion as those residing in Great Britain.

Chapter V

1. Sir Edward Coke (1552–1634) was, inter alia, the prosecutor of Sir Walter Raleigh and, after 1606, the chief justice of common pleas. A champion of the common law, he was also an opponent of the Stuarts. His *Reports* were a standard reference on common law cases for generations.

2. Berkeley (1608–1677) was knighted by Charles I at Berwick and served as governor of Virginia from 1642 to 1652 and again from 1600 until his death. His policies favoring large landowners caused the successful uprising of 1676 led by Nathaniel Bacon. Berkeley clearly met the description of colonial governors given by Postgate in Chapter II. Berkeley is quoted, without further attribution, by Charles and Mary Beard on page 185 of *The Rise of American Civilization* (1927).

3. In order to finance their operations during various French and Indian wars, the legislatures of both Massachusetts and New York had

imposed their own Stamp Acts prior to the distasteful imposition from Parliament. That of Massachusetts lasted for two years from 1755 and that of New York for three years from 1757.

4. Keimer (1688–1739), a native of London, arrived in Philadelphia in 1722 (after bankruptcy in 1715 and deserting his wife in 1721). The entry in the *Dictionary of American Biography* summarizes him as "a negligible person, maundering, frowsy and incompetent...."

5. By the end of nine months, Keimer's subscription list had dwindled to only ninety.

6. This was not a very difficult appointment to secure — he had the only press in the colony.

Chapter VI

1. Peter Stuyvesant (1610–1672) had gone home to the Netherlands following the cession of his province of Nieuw Amsterdam, but eventually returned to live out his days in the English province of New York. One of his final acts as governor, however, had been to promulgate an ordinance restricting the freedom of worship of his subjects. In this regard, Stuyvesant appears to have been a bigot worthy of his days. In 1652, he wrote to the directors of the Dutch West India Company (his employers) requesting that "no Jews be allowed to infest New Netherlands." In this position he was rebuked by his board, but his mindset remained unchanged. Despite Stuyvesant's anti–Semitic leanings, a Jewish synagogue was shown on the 1695 map of New York City. Some of the Livingston land holdings still remain in family hands, three hundred years after their acquisition.

Cadwallader Colden (1688–1776), botanist, physician, historian and scholar was a correspondent with and close rival to Benjamin Franklin as the colonial "Renaissance man." He was surveyor general of New York after 1720 on the Council from 1721 to 1776 and Lieutenant governor after 1761. Occasionally unpopular with a number of radicals, he nevertheless inspired their respect.

2. This land, all in Dutchess County, had been formally ceded on 14 May 1731. It soon became a notorious hangout for counterfeiters.

3. Despite the king's specific instructions that Cosby take no presents from the colonial assemblies under him, when that of New York voted him £750 worth of gratitude he was sufficiently vigorous in expressing his disappointment that the amount was raised another £250.

4. Carried forward to present-day currency values, this would represent something on the order of £5,000 or $8,000, a tidy sum.

5. Fort George was the renamed Fort Amsterdam, first built by the Dutch in 1628 and situated at the lower end of the Broad Way, near today's World Trade Center.

6. This body was presided over by the Duke of Newcastle. Thomas Pelham-Holles (1693–1768) was created duke in 1715. In his capacity as secretary for the Board of Trade for twenty-four years after 1724, he was able to use his patronage to provide critical majorities for a series of prime ministers — Walpole, Pelham and even Pitt.

7. Lewis Morris, Jr., father of Gouverneur (1752–1816), married twice — Sarah Gouverneur, of Huguenot ancestry, being the second. This quotation, while typical of Morris' well-educated mind and being thus attributed by several writers, including Charles and Mary Beard, Henry Steele Commager and Samuel Eliot Morrison, is not precisely cited by any; nor does it appear at all in the authoritative, three-volume biography of Morris written in 1831 by Jared Sparks and published in Boston the following year. The statement appears to have come from a conversation held late in life with Dr. John Wakefield Francis (1789–1861), professor of medicine at Columbia and founder of the New York Academy of Medicine.

8. Daniel Pulteney (d. 1731) was a member of Parliament after 1720 and an ongoing political foe of Walpole, even though the latter had appointed him a lord of the Admiralty in 1721.

9. Some references indicate that Hamilton was eighty years of age at the time of the Zenger trial, but this is not born out by the other dates in his curriculum vitae.

10. The Stamp Act imposed a tax of three pence for the stamps to be affixed to every sheet of every document of legal significance — diplomas, wills, deeds, court pleadings, commercial agreements — even newspapers.

Chapter VII

1. Luzern, Schwyz, Unterwalden and Uri were the participating cantons in this midsummer encounter a few kilometers northwest of Luzern. The Austrian army, under Duke Leopold was equipped with longer spears than the Swiss and could thus hold the Swiss at bay. One volunteer was needed for the suicidal mission of grasping as many of these spears as possible to form a gap in the otherwise impenetrable line. Von Winkelried stepped forward to the heroic task, his final words being recorded as "Take care of my wife and children!"

2. In this chapter and in the four which follow, the extensive quotations are those offered by Zenger himself mostly in the *New York Weekly Journal's* forty-page folio report (June 1736) of the trial entitled *A Brief Narrative of the Case and Trial of John Peter Zenger* (cited in the text as *Narrative*). That issue was widely reprinted, after the fashion of the day — international copyright laws did not go into effect until the end of the nineteenth century — and has become the stuff of legend in the trade of journalism.

In addition to the several editions listed in the Bibliography and referenced in this text, the "Case and Trial" was republished in 1940 as a WPA Writers' project. A shorter (ten-page) account of the trial can be found in the *Manual of the Common Council of New York* for 1856.

3. This quotation is hard to find as such, but in Cicero's *De Natura Deorum* (I. xliv), one can find the phrase "deinde si maxime talis est deus ut nulla gratia nulla hominum caritate teneatur, valeat." This would translate freely as "If (these) friends are such that they are bound by no benevolence, no affection towards men, (then) farewell (to them)."

4. The provenance of this illustration is cloudy. The picture appears in Konkle's life of Andrew Hamilton with an indication that it might have been done by Hintermeister and that the original painting was in the collection of Joseph E. Fayles. It also appears on page 161 of *LAW — A Treasury of Art and Literature* (Levin Associates, 1990), but no credit is given. Both the New York Historical Society and the Frick Museum Reference Archives have been unable to assist in clarification. Hintermeister (1897–1972) was a native of New York, primarily known for his watercolors.

5. Fifty years later, Hawkins was superseded as the standard reference on English law, by the *Commentaries* of William Blackstone.

6. Burnet, bishop of Salisbury after 1689, was staunchly Protestant, but reproved Charles II on his dissolute lifestyle and was forced to flee the country on the accession of James II. Very influential at court under Mary, he was also a thorough researcher and historian.

Burnet's son, William, served as governor of the combined colonies of New York and New Jersey in the years 1720 to 1728. He was also an amateur glaciologist and visited the glaciers of Grindelwald in 1708.

Chapter VIII

1. London, with a population then of almost 800,000, was larger than any three of the colonies combined.

2. Rutgers had been a member of the January 1734 grand jury that had refused to bring an indictment against Zenger. Man had been elected an assistant alderman in 1737. Bell may have been an alternate and known to Zenger, but his name is not in the court records as a juror. Marschalk had been elected an assistant alderman in 1727. Van Borsom had been elected an assistant alderman in 1729. Keteltas had served as an assistant alderman from 1703 through 1709. With the exception of Wendover, whose son became a member of the Continental Congress, all these "good men and true" played no further part in American history.

3. Richard Bradley was attorney general for the province of New York from 1723 until his death in 1752.

4. In later years this would be called a stipulation.

Chapter IX

1. Here "The Provinces" refers not only to Providence Plantations but also to the province of New York.

2. Cosby reported to the Board of Trade, chaired by the Duke of Newcastle, not directly to the King or Parliament.

3. Sir John Holt (1642–1710), a counselor and Whig Member of Parliament. An opponent of standing armies, he became Lord Chief Justice in 1689 and was widely noted for his fairness towards all accused who were brought before him for trial. John Tutchin (1661–1707), a Whig pamphleteer, published *The Observator* after 1702. Because of his unwelcome custom of exposing scandals, a bill was brought against him "to restrain the licentiousness of the press." He was tried and found guilty, but the verdict was set aside on appeal — a point that Bradley ignored. Holt had earlier defined the crime in the following words: "Anything written of another which holds him up to scorn and ridicule, or might reasonably be considered as provoking him to a breach of the peace, is a libel."

4. This citation dealt with William Fuller (1670–1717), a friend and associate of the imaginative Titus Oates (of "Popish Plot" fame). Fuller also "knew" much about Jacobite and other treasonous conspiracies and printed numerous tracts, as well as some spurious letters allegedly written by James II, to prove the validity of his charges.

Chapter X

1. A case prosecuted before the House of Lords, wherein seven bishops, led by William Sancroft (1617–1693) Archbishop of Canterbury, refused to promulgate a Declaration of Indulgence from their pulpits. This was a decree whereby King James II proposed to grant complete freedom of worship to all his subjects. The bishops argued — successfully — that the king was attempting to dispense a power that he did not possess.

Chapter XI

1. John Hampden (1594–1643) achieved considerable respect for his forthrightness in opposing the payment of any tax not duly authorized by

Parliament. A Puritan and a leading member of Parliament, Hampden refused to pay the "ship money" demanded of him by King Charles I. Hampden later died of wounds suffered at the Battle of Chalgrove Field in the Civil War. A hero to Puritans generally, his name was placed on the land in several New England locations.

2. Norris (1660–1749), known as "Foulweather Jack," had been appointed commander-in-chief of the Royal Navy on 20 February 1733 and was the first commander to fly the "Union Jack." He had two sons, both of whom also served in the Royal Navy. The younger, Harry, served with distinction, achieving the rank of vice-admiral by the time of his death in 1764. The elder, Richard, held the rank of captain, but was cashiered after showing cowardice in the face of the French enemy on 11 February 1734; six weeks later, his father decided to retire as commander in chief "for the good of the service." Biographers have neglected to verify any relationship between Norris and Morris.

3. Freely translated these lines could be read 250 years later as:
> Laws have been measured out. Liberty is help in respect.
> These things at last come forth.
> It (liberty) is procured by courage, not wealth.
> May it thus turn out for each person as he deserved from the republic.

Chapter XII

1. Dickinson (1732–1808) was a lawyer and delegate from Pennsylvania to the Continental Congress. His letters attacked the Townshend Acts and were widely reprinted in colonial newspapers. Hoping for reconciliation with England, he refused to sign the Declaration of Independence, but he did become a framer of the Constitution, the adoption of which he urged in another series of letters. Dickinson College in Carlyle, Pennsylvania is named in his honor.

2. This event had been delayed by Zenger's imprisonment; it had been approved by the aldermen and mayor on 25 October 1734.

3. After Zenger's death, Anna lived near Harmanus Rutgers and continued to sell printed items from her home.

4. Zenger's obituary was also carried in the 4 August 1746 issue of the *New York Weekly Journal.*

5. Sir William Blackstone (1723–1780) was a failure in the practice of law, but is remembered to this day for his scholarly summation, *Commentaries on the Law of England.* As the name of Nathaniel Bowditch has become synonymous with nautical navigation, so that of Blackstone has taken a position with respect to the law.

6. McDougall (1731–1786), a native of the Inner Hebrides, was a vigorous opponent of the restrictions applied by Parliament against American trade. He became a general in the War for Independence and was a twice a member of Congress.

7. Fox (1749–1806) was the foremost liberal thinker of his day in English politics. In a series of cabinet positions, he opposed repressive measures against the colonies, opposed the slave trade, urged emancipation for Roman Catholics, and reform of judicial procedures.

8. Campbell (1779–1861) became Lord Chief Justice in 1850 and Lord Chancellor in 1859. An influential figure of English politics, he also brought about reform of the real estate laws and urged recognition of the Confederacy during the American Civil War. He wrote the authoritative *Lives of the Lord Chancellors* and *Lives of the Lord Chief Justices*.

9. Meager (1823–1867) escaped in 1852 and made it to the United States where he became a Union general in the Civil War. He drowned while on his way to assume office as the second territorial governor of Montana. O'Brien (1803–1864), a lineal descendant of the legendary Brian Boru, was released in 1854 and died, ill and forgotten ten years later in Bangor, Wales. Mitchell (1815–1875), a lawyer by training, escaped to New York in 1853 where he founded another partisan newspaper. He returned to Ireland in 1874 and was promptly elected to Parliament, but was equally promptly declared ineligible to serve.

10. Slavery does receive three oblique mentions in the Constitution.

11. Hale (1609–1676) served under both Cromwell and King Charles II. At the time of his death he was chief judge of the Court of King's Bench.

12. Wirt (1772–1834), born in Maryland, was admitted to the Virginia bar in 1790 and later served in the commonwealth's legislature.

13. Piatt (1819–1891), the son of Judge Jacob Wycoff Piatt, was this author's great, great, great uncle.

Chapter XIII

1. General von der Tann (1815–1881) later served the Prussian victors with considerable distinction. Ludwig August von Benedek (1804–1881), von der Tann's Austrian counterpart, fared worse; he was court martialed and cashiered because of his army's inept showing.

2. These three were the signers of the multinational Treaty of Paris on 3 September 1783, by which the independence of the United States was acknowledged by various European nations — most importantly, Great Britain.

3. New York was a laggard in this respect, not finally outlawing the slave trade until 1827. However, its provincial assembly had decreed in 1758 that the children of Negro slaves were emancipated at age twenty-one.

4. The total 1790 population (including Vermont, the southwest region, and the Northwest Territory) was 3,929,214.

5. In the Reconstruction Era, there were ample sympathetic majorities in enough state legislatures to assure quick ratification of the Thirteenth, Fourteenth and Fifteenth Amendments.

6. William Lloyd Prosser (d. 1972), a professor of law, saw this comprehensive legal textbook through four editions by himself. This quotation is taken from a subsequent fifth edition, done in collaboration with Keeton.

Chapter XIV

1. From the graduation program of Dartmouth College, June 1918. The introduction by President Ernest Martin Hopkins cited Simonds as a *"distinguished son of Harvard University, journalist, soldier in the Spanish-American War, illuminating critic of current military affairs ..."*

2. Frank would tell the credulous that it was his grandfather. However, the line of paternal descent is clear in the records of the New England Historical Genealogical Society — Joshua, Jr. (b. 1736); William (b. 1774); Eli (b. 1817); William Henry (b. 1844). They all lived in Lexington, however.

There were three Simonds among the 141 men on the Lexington muster roll. Joseph (b. 1740) was an ensign. Joshua, who married Martha Bowers in 1765, was a common soldier who actually took part in the first skirmish and then helped John Lowell and Paul Revere remove to safety a trunkful of incriminating papers belonging to Sam Adams and John Hancock.

3. Our old friend, Andrew John Kauffman II writes: "I know Frank; he guided me, my father and the Hungarian minister, John Pelenyi, on a memorable and fact-loaded visit to Manassas, opening his words with: '*I propose not to discuss the First Battle of Bull Run, because it consisted mostly not so much of a real show of arms as little more than two mobs going at one another, with the least undisciplined winning the day.*' So we discussed Second Manassas, with Simonds telling us what an idiot General Pope was, and how Jackson, rushing east from the Shenandoah, arrived just in time to save Lee's bacon, or Pope would have won by sheer strength of numbers despite his obvious incompetence."

4. Katherine became Mrs. Lovell Thompson, and James Gledhill became a newswriter before turning to forestry.

5. The famous editor and owner of the *Sun*, Charles Anderson Dana, had died in 1897.

6. Henri-Philippe Pétain (1856–1951), the most heroic and tragic figure of twentieth century history, was one of the few French generals with real compassion for the common soldier. A hero of World War I, he was

made a marshal of France for his services. However, his "collaboration" with the Germans after the French defeat of 1940 ultimately led to his imprisonment.

7. Throughout his life, Simonds seldom had a good word for the British. In part this may have been his heritage from his ancestor, Joshua; in other part, it may have been justified by more recent impressions. In any case, the government of England was conspicuous by its absence from the list.

8. In all fairness to the Germans, submarine warfare was already a known fact of the conflict, and the German consulate had run notices in the New York newspapers for several days in advance of the *Lusitania* sailing warning that the ship was carrying military supplies and would be treated as such. This was, of course, vehemently denied by the British, and it was not until another half-century had passed before unequivocal proof of this fact came to the surface when divers retrieved cases of armaments from the ship's cargo.

9. From *Pulitzer Prize Editorials* by W. David Sloan (Ames: Iowa State University Press, 1980, p. 3).

10. Arthur Hendrick Vandenberg (1884–1951), another newspaperman, was appointed to the Senate in 1928 and reelected to three subsequent terms. Though of the minority party, he was designated by President Truman to be the United States' delegate to the founding meeting of the United Nations in 1945.

11. The neighboring Dominion of Canada was in the war from the outset, though its populace also included a substantial minority group of Germanic ancestry. While heroic on the part of its British majority, Canada's war effort was hampered by the isolationism of its large French-speaking minority, a condition that continues to hamstring Canadian affairs.

12. Foremost among these was the second Pulitzer-Prize-winning editorialist, Henry Watterson of the *Louisville Courier-Journal*.

13. Written in collaboration with Brooks Emeny, later to be president of the Foreign Policy Association, this was published in 1935 and reprinted in 1937 after Simonds's death.

14. The house has been converted to a pleasant country caravanserai (Snowvillage Inn), which enjoys a magnificent panoramic view of the Presidential Range, some twenty miles distant to the northwest, and whose current owners still maintain Simonds memorabilia in respectful evidence.

15. The etymological definition is even more complex, deriving from the Armenian word *vilayet*, meaning a province or subdivision of a nation. In World War I, a soldier receiving a serious wound was sent "back to Blighty"; hence such a wound became known as a "blighty."

16. These lectures, with a most informative introduction, were printed as *American Foreign Policy in the Post-War Years* (Baltimore: Johns Hopkins University Press, 1935).

17. The Central Powers in 1914 consisted of Germany, Austria-Hungary, Turkey and Bulgaria.

18. Simonds died of pneumonia in Washington, D.C., on 23 January 1936.

19. This was the agreement of August 843, by which the Carolingian Empire was divided among the surviving sons of Louis the Pious — Charles the Bald, Louis the German and Lothair I.

Chapter XV

1. Taking a legal appeal as far as the United States Supreme Court is not a casual undertaking and can run into many hundreds of thousands of dollars.

2. Taken — as are all the following quotations — from *U.S. Supreme Court Reports* (11 L. ed. 2d 686 *infra*).

3. Some of the charges made in the advertisement had occurred prior to Sullivan's tenure as police commissioner; the students sang the National Anthem, not "My Country 'Tis of Thee;" there was no lockout of the dining hall; King had been arrested only four times, not seven; though present in large numbers, the police did not "ring" the campus.

4. Lester B. Sullivan (1921–1977) continued in public employment after this suit was concluded. At the time of his death in Tallassee, he was executive assistant to the Alabama attorney general and had previously been the state's public safety director and prison commissioner.

5. An excellent summary of the American law on libel (as it stood on that date) can be found in the same edition as the original reference on *New York Times v. Sullivan* (376 U.S. 254, 11 L. ed. 2d 686, S. Ct. 710) starting on page 1116.

6. Emphasis is the author's.

Appendix B

1. Old Style.

2. This language is convoluted, but the intent was to make sure neither of the "Pretenders" could qualify. George I (1660–1727), the first member of the House of Hanover, was a great-grandson of James I, and therefore had a claim to legitimacy in succession when Queen Anne died childless.

3. A dispensation from the crown to do a thing notwithstanding any statute to the contrary.

Appendix D

1. Giving authority to its permanence, this document was reaffirmed by the Constitution of the French Fourth Republic in 1958.

2. The Estates General corresponded to the Medieval English Parliament and was only occasionally convened by French kings. The First of the Estates General, was the upper members of the Clergy. The Second was the Nobility. Both of them together numbered collectively something like 1 percent of the Third Estate, the lesser privileged classes (bourgeoisie). There was no "estate" for the common people. Some time later, the "Press" constituted itself as the Fourth Estate.

Bibliography

Freedom of the press is such a popular subject that a complete listing of words written about it would hardly be possible. Material dealing specifically with John Peter Zenger, on the other hand, is not to be found on most public library bookshelves. The titles I have found most useful in this endeavor are given here. A more extensive list of Zenger-related material can be found in Buranelli's *The Trial of Peter Zenger.*

Alexander, James. *A Brief Narrative of the Case and Trial of John Peter Zenger, Printer of the New York Weekly Journal.* Ed. Stanley Nider Katz. Cambridge, Mass.: Harvard University Press, 1963.

American Dictionary of Printing and Bookmaking. New York: Howard Lockwood, 1894.

Bleyer, William Grosvenor. *Main Currents in the History of American Journalism.* New York: Da Capo Press, 1973.

Bogen, David S. *Origins of Freedom of Speech and Press. Maryland Law Review* 42:429 [contains much material on Trenchard and Gordon — "Cato"].

Bollinger, Lee C. *The Tolerant Society: Freedom of Speech and Extremist Speech in America.* Oxford University Press, 1986.

_____. *Images of a Free Press.* Chicago: University of Chicago Press, 1991.

Buranelli, Vincent. *The Trial of Peter Zenger.* New York: New York University Press, 1957 [offers an excellent "Suggestions for Further Reading"].

Bury, John Bagnell. *History of Freedom of Thought.* New York: Holt, 1913.

Cheslaw, I. *John Peter Zenger and His "New York Weekly Journal."* New York: Zenger Memorial Fund, 1952.

Cobb, Sanford Hoadley. *The Rise of Religious Liberty in America.* New York: Macmillan, 1902.

Colden, Cadwallader. *History of William Cosby's Administration as Governor of the Province of New York, and of Lieutenant-Governor George Clarke's Administration Through 1737.* New York: N.Y. State Historical Society Collections, 1935.

Defoe, Daniel. *A Brief History of the Poor Palatine Refugees Lately Arrived in England.* London: 1709 [available as publication 106 of the Augustan Reprint Society, New York].

Gibson, Michael T. *The Supreme Court and Freedom of Expression from 1791 to 1917. Fordham Law Review* 55:263 [constitutes a good resource on the evolution of press freedom after Zenger].

Hildeburn, Charles, S. R. *Sketches of Printers and Printing in Colonial New York.* New York: Dodd, Mead, 1895.

Hudson, Frederic. *Journalism in the United States from 1690 to 1872.* New York: Harper & Brothers, 1873.

Hurwitz, Leon. *Historical Dictionary of Censorship in the United States.* Westport, Conn.: Greenwood, 1986.

Knightley, Phillip. *The First Casualty.* New York and London: Harcourt Brace Jovanovich, 1975.

Konkle, Burton Alva. *The Life of Andrew Hamilton.* Philadelphia: National Publishing, 1941.

McAffee, Thomas B., et al. *The Bill of Rights, Social Contract Theory, and the Rights "Retained" by the People. Southern Illinois Law Journal* 16:267 [contains several articles on the historic perspective of free speech].

Noel, Dix W. *Defamation of Public Officials and Candidates. Columbia Law Review* 49:875.

Rossiter, Clinton L. *1787: The Grand Convention.* New York: Macmillan, 1966 [a fact-filled analysis of the framers and the Constitutional Convention].

Rutherfurd, Livingston. *John Peter Zenger, His Press, His Trial and a Bibliography of Zenger Imprints.* New York: Dodd, Mead, 1904.

Thomas, Isaiah. *The History of Printing in America, with a Biography of Printers and an Account of Newspapers.* Worcester, Mass.: J. Munsell, 1810.

Weinberger, Harry. *The Liberty of the Press.* Two addresses at the time of unveiling of two tablets commemorating the services of Andrew Hamilton in defense of John Peter Zenger. Berkeley Heights, N.J.: Oride.

Useful citations for the more pertinent legal cases in the evolution of press and speech freedoms in the United States prior to *New York Times v. Sullivan* are:

City of Chicago v. Tribune Co. 307 Ill. 595, 607, 139 N.E. 86, 90 (1923)

Charles Parker Co. v. Silver City Crystal Co. 142 Conn. 605, 618, 116 A.2d 440 (1955)

Phoenix Newspapers v. Choisser. 82 Ariz. 271, 277, 312 P.2d 150 (1957)

N.A.A.C.P. v. Button. 371 U.S. 415, 433, 9 L. Ed. 2d 405
Bridges v. California. 314 U.S. 252, 270, 86 L. Ed. 192

There are several books dealing with the migrations of the Palatines after 1709 that can be found in many reference libraries. Among the more informative are those by Henry Z. Jones, Walter Allen Knittle, Eula C. Lapp, Roland Paul and A. G. Roeber.

One can read the full text of Zenger's *Narrative* in many places, but among the more intriguing is the fifty-nine-page reprint of 1765 by J. Almon, which also includes a narrative of the inconclusive trial in 1764 of William Owen, a London bookseller.

Index